PINK UP YOUR LIFE!

Manuela Roth

PINK UP YOUR LIFE!

THE WORLD OF PINK DESIGN

BRAUN

Contents

Preface

"Pink, it was love at first sight - Yeah, pink when I turn out the light... Pink it's the color of passion" - so Aerosmith tell us in their song "Pink". Pink divides people like almost no other color. Some love it and can't get enough of it. They want to surround themselves with pink clothes and accessories and pink decoration while others see it as the image for small, cute girls - too sweet to take it seriously.

Our societies instill this attitude in us, as they try to shoehorn us into predetermined gender roles. Men are assigned strong colors like blue and black and design that is grand and angular. For women, everything seems to be a little softer, smaller and prettier, often in one of thousands of shades of red and pink. The allocation of roles seems obvious.

Yet in the middle ages, pink as a shade of red was a strong color that was denied to the powerful only. And only a hundred years ago, pink - as the "small red" - was the color for boys as it was perceived as stronger and therefore more suitable for the male sex. Girls were dressed in delicate shades of blue and their rooms decorated in pale blue.

Pink is not just pink: there is an unlimited number of hues ranging from delicate and classy dusky pink to shocking pink and neon shades. The color suggests naivety and romance on the one hand and energy and passion, radiance and glamor on the other. In nature, many plants have pink petals that seem fresh and delicate and convey life, energy and beauty.

Pink is a particular favorite color among designers, signifying optimism, energy and intangibility. The products presented in this book, taken from all aspects of everyday life, are surprising in their vitality and sometimes also in their humor. Pink is particularly conspicuous and the vast array of basic commodities available in pink, and presented here alongside products for children, is therefore no surprise. The color naturally plays a role in the world of fashion, but it is the pink vehicles, the pink gadgets targeted at both genders and above all the pink public places that especially command our attention.

The designer Karim Rashid has made a notable commitment to the color pink. As an industrial designer, he has already created almost every conceivable interior fixture and piece of furniture, always for the biggest companies and brands. He has designed over 3,000 products and received more than 300 prizes. His products can be seen in the permanent collections of more than 20 art galleries and museums around the world. A trailblazing designer, he loves to wear pink himself and GQ Magazine once said that he has made the color masculine. Several of his products are featured in this book, from a kitchen design for the manufacturer Gorenje and a fitted bathroom in pink, to a perfume bottle with a sensual design.

Of course, every other designer presented here has also deliberately chosen to use the color pink - not only to define the target group but also to convey emotions. For example, the timeless, simple and beautiful chair from Arne Jacobsen's Series 7, originally designed 60 years ago, has been produced in a special pale pink version to celebrate the jubilee.

The perfume Joop! Homme was first launched in 1989 and has been a classic among fragrances for men ever since. Right from the beginning, it has been sold in pink packaging with a pink bottle! The personalized addition of some pink parts lends extra class to the Harley Davidson Forty-Eight, a classic among motorbikes, while a classic Swiss pocket-knife acquires a contemporary look through its transparent pink casing. In our built environments and in public spaces pink is also used to catch the eye and convey positive emotions. The patisserie Zumbo in Melbourne, for example, is bathed in pink light, which casts a glow over the walls, ceiling and furniture, but without a hint of kitsch.

Don your rose-tinted glasses and browse through the world before you, filled with wonderful pink products. Pick out your favorite shade of pink from the 100 plus products and projects. There's a pink for everyone among the myriad shades. Let yourself be seduced and inspired, astounded and amused!

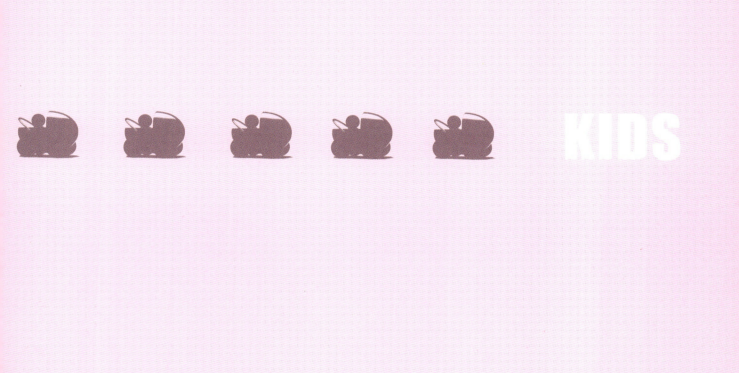

KIDS

BIOBU /
Bambino Kids' Collection

Designed for everyday use, at home, or on the move, the Bambino Kids' Collection comprises a range of alternative dinnerware that is practical, durable and environmentally friendly. The range is envisaged as an alternative to traditional plastic, disposable or fragile dishware. To extend the life of the products, the designers combined biodegradable bamboo fiber, a renewable natural resource, with a 100% food-grade melamine binder. The range comprises cups, bowls, plates and trays, all in a variety of sizes including smaller sets designed for use by children. A variety of color choices are available, including rose, a soft but vibrant shade of pink.

PRODUCER: Boo Louis for EKOBO
YEAR OF DEVELOPMENT: 2013
MAIN MATERIAL: bamboo fiber

Blabla Kids Dolls

Blabla was founded in 2001 by Susan Pritchett and Florence Wetterwald, who had recently visited Peru and been inspired by the villages of expert knitters keeping the tradition alive. Blabla now employs these Peruvian knitters to hand knit every product. Central to the company's ethos are fair trade and environmental considerations. Melody, Confetti and Giselle are three of the knitted dolls available from Blabla. Each has its own story: Melody likes cold showers and sardine butter, while Confetti is the life of the party and Giselle is an Irish line dancer. All of the dolls and other products, including the Hold Me Tight Smile Pillow, are 100% cotton. The soft pink thread used in the items featured here is notable for its calming hue.

DESIGN: Florence Wetterwald
PRODUCER: Blabla Kids
YEAR OF DEVELOPMENT: 2012
MAIN MATERIAL: 100% cotton

Florence Wetterwald

Toy Baskets

Products made of raffia have long been a firm fixture in RICE's catalogue. These toy baskets with handsewn details add to this long tradition. The raffia fibers are sourced from palm trees in Madagascar. Over three hundred native families are then involved in the production of RICE's raffia products, all of which are made by hand. Raffia is a natural substance and varies in color, making each product unique. RICE's colored products are created without the use of potentially dangerous chemicals. RICE is a Danish homewares and accessories company and was founded in 1998 by Charlotte Hedeman Gueniau.

DESIGN: Charlotte Hedeman Gueniau
PRODUCER: RICE
YEAR OF DEVELOPMENT: 2014
MAIN MATERIAL: raffia fibers

Charlotte Hedeman Gueniau

Bobby-Car-Classic Girlie

The BIG-Bobby-Car-Classic Girlie in bright pink was developed for girls from 12 months. The car's body is designed in accordance with child ergonomics and features an easy-grip steering wheel, four sturdy wheels and a knee recess for older children. Ackermann steering makes a small turning circle possible, while the low center of gravity prevents the Bobby-Car-Classic Girlie from tipping over at any speed. A matching trailer can be attached to the trailer couplings on the front and rear of the car. The car is manufactured according to ultramodern production methods in a high-tech plant in Germany.

PRODUCER: BIG-SPIELWARENFABRIK
YEAR OF DEVELOPMENT: 2012
MAIN MATERIAL: polyethylene (PE)

mini micro sporty

Developed in collaboration with specialist doctors from Switzerland, the mini micro is designed to enhance the movement, motor function and coordination of the child through its weight control. The footboard, reinforced with glass fiber, is made of soft synthetic material with the aim of preventing injury and the wheels are manufactured from hard rubber. It is intended for use by children aged 2 to 5 and primarily on asphalt surfaces. The handlebars can be removed to allow for easy transportation in a car or suitcase. The combination of dark and light shades of pink makes the mini micro particularly attractive. Micro is a Swiss company founded in 1996 that develops and produces mobility products for children, teenagers and adults.

PRODUCER: Micro Mobility Systems
YEAR OF DEVELOPMENT: 2001
MAIN MATERIAL: glass fiber reinforced plastic, aluminum

GHOST Powerkid 20

The GHOST Powerkid 20 is the lightest in the series and has an optmized aluminum frame for improved performance. It features Shimano gears and a Tektro V-Brake. The available color combinations include blue and red, black and red, limegreen and blue, and pink and white, the last of which is especially striking. The bike is one of four in the Powerkid series, ranging from 12 inch to 24 inch. GHOST is a German bicycle manufacturer that also offers a full range of cycling accessories.

PRODUCER: GHOST-Bikes
YEAR OF DEVELOPMENT: 2015
MAIN MATERIAL: aluminum frame

bObles

The story of bObles began in 2006, when the two sisters and mothers, architect Bolette Blædel and designer Louise Blædel, started designing multifunctional tumbling furniture for children. Out of a personal dream of creating quality design for children, which both stimulates and develops, grew a business that within a few years had transformed itself into an international brand. Based on abstract animal shapes and geometric forms, the tumbling furniture has a Scandinavian, minimalistic look. The different pieces are manufactured in solid EVA-foam without any dangerous phthalates, with a soft surface which can be easily cleaned. The material is light and the edges are rounded so the furniture does not leave any marks in the floor. Combining multiple dark and light shades, the pink color option is suitable for any child.

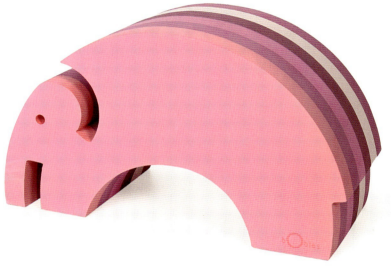

DESIGN: Bolette Blædel, Louise Blædel
PRODUCER: bObles
YEAR OF DEVELOPMENT: 2006
MAIN MATERIAL: EVA-foam

Grand Piano

The Hape grand piano is intended for children interested in making music. Its 30-note keyboard is the ideal size for small hands. The piano is made mostly of wood, but incorporates some metal and is painted with polyurethane paint. Hape believes in the positive influence of music-making for developing children's creative powers. This piano enables children to explore sounds and music in a fun and stimulating way. Hape Toys is one of the world's largest producers of toys made from sustainable materials. From the beginning of the design process, through production and delivery, to the final unwrapping of the consumer packaging, Hape toys are a collaboration of global thinking and responsible ecology.

PRODUCER: Hape International
YEAR OF DEVELOPMENT: 2013
MAIN MATERIAL: wood

i-Woody

The i-Woody is intended for use by young children not yet old enough to have their first real smartphone. Made of wood and accompanied by chalk and a sponge for writing and erasing messages on the smartphone's face, the i-Woody is designed as a fun and ecologically-friendly toy. It also comes with a set of headphones for added realism.

Designed by Donkey, the toy is one of many innovative products to emerge from the company's creative team. Inspired by everyday items, they seek to create extraordinary products that can be found nowhere else. They create products that tell stories, entertain and elicit joy in those who use them.

PRODUCER: Donkey Products
YEAR OF DEVELOPMENT: 2010
MAIN MATERIAL: wood

Mini Clouds Wallstickers

These wallstickers by ferm LIVING are made of vinyl and are intended to decorate interior spaces. They can be applied to all even and smooth surfaces but not rough surfaces such as brick walls. The 27 neon pink stickers in the shape of clouds of different sizes can be arranged as the user wishes.

Ferm LIVING draws on Scandinavian design traditions and imbues them with a contemporary graphic edge. Founded in Denmark by Trine Anderson in 2005, the studio soon expanded into design and interior products including wallpaper, cushions and furniture.

PRODUCER: ferm LIVING
YEAR OF DEVELOPMENT: 2013
MAIN MATERIAL: vinyl

Fjällräven Kånken

The Kånken backpack was launched in 1978 to help prevent back problems among Swedish school children. Kånken Kids is a smaller version of the now classic design. It has straps that are specifically designed to fit a small child's back and a chest strap with reflector to hold the shoulder straps in place. It also features a

removable sitting pad stored in the inside back pocket. Made from durable and light Vinylon F fabric, the backpack is resistant to dirt and water. The main compartment has a large zippered opening, while two flat pockets on the side and a front pocket with zipper offer additional storage. There are many colors available including peach pink.

DESIGN: Åke Nordin
PRODUCER: Fjällräven
YEAR OF DEVELOPMENT: 1978
MAIN MATERIAL: Vinylon F

Åke Nordin

Eames Elephant

In 1945, Charles and Ray Eames designed a toy elephant made from plywood but it was never mass produced. This modern version is made from colored plastic (dyed-through polypropylene) and has a matt finish. It can be used indoors or outdoors as a robust toy or as a decorative object in a child's room. The Eames Elephant is available in five colors: white, ice gray, classic red, dark lime and light pink. Charles and Ray Eames are two of the most renowned personalities of the twentieth century in the world of design. Among other endeavors, they have designed furniture, made films and conceived exhibitions. Vitra is the only legitimate manufacturer of their products for Europe and the Middle East.

DESIGN: Charles & Ray Eames
PRODUCER: Vitra
YEAR OF DEVELOPMENT: 1945
MAIN MATERIAL: polypropylene

maxi micro coral

The Maxi Micro kickboard is designed for children aged from five to twelve who are too big for the Mini Micro but still too small for kickboards. It comes in various metallic shades including blue, camo green, purple and pink. Its inbuilt weight control ensures stability for the rider. The wheels are made of hard rubber and are most suitable for asphalt surfaces. The handlebars are height-adjustable and can also be removed and replaced by a stick with knobs if this is preferable. Micro Scooter is based in Switzerland and seeks to produce high-quality products that meet the mobility, fitness and fashion needs of the modern urban lifestyle.

PRODUCER: Micro Mobility Systems
YEAR OF DEVELOPMENT: 2006
MAIN MATERIAL: glass fiber reinforced plastic, aluminum

CUBE Kid 200

The CUBE Kid 200 in pink'n'white'n'blue combines a basic pink frame with white mounted parts and is intended for use by girls. It features a strong but light heat-treated 6061 aluminum frame and V-brakes at the front and rear which offer ample stopping power for trail-riding and are activated by levers specifically sized for children's hands.

A power modulator unit on the front brake prevents the bike from going into an unwanted nose-wheelie, while the Shimano 7-speed shifting with Revo twist shifter is designed to make gear changing easy. Suitable accessories by CUBE include the Junior Softshell Jacket, the Junior Backpack and the Junior Race Gloves.

DESIGN: Alexandra Pfletscher
PRODUCER: CUBE
YEAR OF DEVELOPMENT: 2014
MAIN MATERIAL: aluminum

Alexandra Pfletscher

Rebel Kidz Trainer Bike

The Rebel Kidz wooden bike features a high-quality, comfortable, retro saddle and handlebars with protection against collisions. It has 12-inch five-spoke EVA wheels and pneumatic tires. The saddle has three height positions between 32 and 36 centimeters. The bike comes in seven different stylish color designs including "black flames", "blue/orange" and with pink butterflies. It is intended for use by children aged between two and five years and can carry a maximum weight of 35 kilograms. Rebel Kidz design and manufacture bikes for children in wood and steel, each in several sizes, as well as offering safety helmets in a variety of designs.

PRODUCER: Project Sports
YEAR OF DEVELOPMENT: 2013
MAIN MATERIAL: birch plywood

PHOTOS: COURTESY OF THE PRODUCER

PLAYSAM Toys

As the leading Scandinavian design company in its class, PLAYSAM creates innovative and timeless Swedish wooden toys for the young and the young at heart. With each and every toy, they not only strive for physical functionality, but also for an art form that challenges pre-existing artistic concepts and conventions. Extraordinary sleek, these wooden toys made of European beech wood, and coated numerous times with certified toxin-free lacquer paing, beg to be touched, handled and played with.

PRODUCER: PLAYSAM
YEAR OF DEVELOPMENT: 2006 (above),
1984 (left), 2008 (b. l.), 2009 (b. r.)
MAIN MATERIAL: wood, metal, plastic

Hoptimist

The Hoptimists were originally created by Danish cabinetmaker Hans Gustav Ehrenreich in 1968-74. He initially designed the famous Birdies and in 1969 the frog Kvak, the girl Bimble and the boy Bumble were created. Bimble is recognizable by her smiling eyes while Bumble's eyes are attentive and inquisitive. Ehrenreich's basic idea was to draw the Hoptimists using a circle and an ellipse - and this is how the classics and the new generation of figurines are still drawn today. Danish designer Lotte Steffensen and her husband Bo founded the company Hoptimist in 2008 and since then the Hoptimists have been relaunched and sold with great success. For Lotte it is important to be as authentic and in the spirit of Ehrenreich as possible. A range of colors is available including yellow, lime copper, oak and pink.

DESIGN: Hans Gustav Ehrenreich
PRODUCER: Hoptimist
YEAR OF DEVELOPMENT: 1968
MAIN MATERIAL: plastic ABS,
copper-plaited plastic

Hans Gustav Ehrenreich, Lotte Steffensen

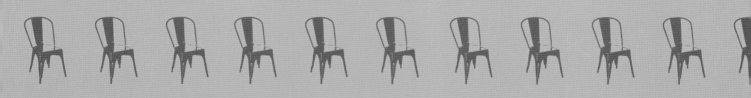

@ HOME

Gorenje Kitchen Collection

The Gorenje collection designed by Karim Rashid comprises a built-in oven with HomeMADE technology, a modern kitchen hood and a cooking hob with unique graphics. The full-length handle is the focal point of the collection, both in terms of appearance and interaction. Using the innovative MoodLite technology developed by Gorenje, the vertical LED light strip allows several color versions, providing the option to adjust the appearance of the appliance to the user's current mood or lifestyle. Pink is just one color option available. The LED strip on the oven offers the desired hue as well as lighting the oven's interior and warning of high temperatures with a red tint.

DESIGN: Karim Rashid
PRODUCER: Gorenje
YEAR OF DEVELOPMENT: 2009
MAIN MATERIAL: brushed aluminum, LED light, glass

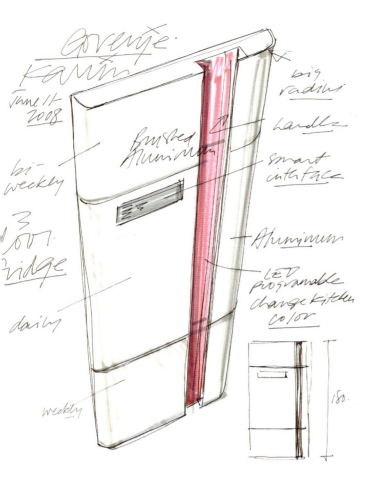

Gorenje.
Karim
June 11 2008

bi-weekly

3 100%.
Fridge

daily

weekly

Brushed Aluminum

big radius

handle

smart interface

Aluminum

LED programable change kitchen color

180.

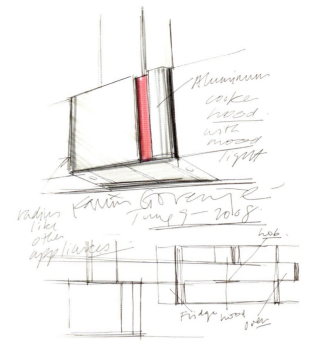

Aluminum cooker hood. with mood light

radius like other appliances

Karim Gorenje June 9 - 2008.

hob.

Fridge hood over

Karim Rashid

fatboy

A decade after its first appearance, the fatboy Original beanbag designed by Jukka Setälä is still a popular item. Its EPS filling allows the beanbag to mold to the user's body while retaining its original shape. Strong nylon fabric was chosen for durability. The Original is available in a wide range of colors including several shades of pink. The Buggle-up, the fatboy's outdoor beanbag, is also available in pink as well as fifteen other colors. Its tough fabric can withstand UV rays, water and dirt, and it is designed to accommodate one or two people. Fatboy was founded in the Netherlands in 2002 and offers, besides a wide range of colorful beanbags, also lamps, sunshades, carpets, hammocks and more.

PRODUCER: Fatboy
YEAR OF DEVELOPMENT: 2009, 2002
MAIN MATERIAL: polyester/nylon with PVC coating, filling EPS

Dot Carpet

Dot Carpet is part of Danish company HAY's accessory and rug collection. The basic notes are simple, but Scholten & Baijings's precise paintbrush cuts through the calm surface with neon-powered patterns. Made of thousands of hand-rolled felt balls sewn together in a geometric pattern, the carpet comes in a variety of colors including hot pink and pink magnolia, the striking colors contrasting the neutral grays. The 100% wool carpet was launched in 2010 and is available in three sizes. Founded in 2002, HAY was created with the vision of reviving the innovative greatness of 1950s and 1960s design in a contemporary context.

Scholten & Baijings

DESIGN: Scholten & Baijings
PRODUCER: HAY
YEAR OF DEVELOPMENT: 2010
MAIN MATERIAL: wool

PHOTOS: COURTESY OF THE PRODUCER, MARIE PIERRE MOREL (PORTRAIT)

Cindy

The Cindy table lamp was inspired by the designs of the 1970s and was created as a contemporary interpretation of vintage lamps. It comprises a conical lampshade and rounded teardrop base and comes in a broad range of metallic tones The lamp's shiny chrome-like finish is its most striking feature. Kartell was founded in 1949 by a young chemical engineer called Giulio Castelli. Originally based in Milan, Kartell's aim was to create products with innovative features that could take advantage of new, more efficient, production techniques. The company has grown ever since and opened its own museum in 1999.

Ferruccio Laviani

DESIGN: Ferruccio Laviani
PRODUCER: KARTELL Spa.
YEAR OF DEVELOPMENT: 2009
MAIN MATERIAL: metallic ABS

Ladykiller Soap

Soap is normally round or square, but this soap by Donkey is shaped like a pistol. It is available in mini or normal size and in two different shades of pink, including pale pink with a rose scent. The item is envisaged as a means of making bathtime more fun. The irony of a harmless, fragrant gun makes this product unique. Donkey started life as a family business in the novelty gift industry. Founder Florian Berger took a detour into design and advertising before returning to his roots.

PRODUCER: Donkey Products
YEAR OF DEVELOPMENT: 2008
MAIN MATERIAL: soap

Paper Jewelry

Each item of paper jewelry from kolor is constructed from three different paper polyhedrons. Comprising two sheets of colored card, each with a shape punched out, the set of decorations can be easily built at home. This involves extricating the shape from the card, folding it, gluing it together and hanging it with a thread as a decoration on a tree or as part of a mobile. Originally conceived as alternative Christmas decorations, these ornaments are also suitable for adorning a home or garden throughout the year. Pink is one of several available colors. Tatjana Reimann and Uli Meyer are the founders of Berlin-based kolor Studio.

kolor

DESIGN: kolor
PRODUCER: kolor Studio für Gestaltung
YEAR OF DEVELOPMENT: 2011
MAIN MATERIAL: cardboard

Swan Sofa

The Swan sofa was first created in 1958 by Arne Jacobsen, whose collaboration with Fritz Hansen dates back to 1934. Asked to design the Royal Hotel in Copenhagen in the late 1950s, Jacobsen created several new products including the Egg and Swan chairs and the Swan sofa. It was in production from 1964 to 1974 and was reintroduced in 2000.

Like the Egg and Swan, the sofa is based on curves and contains no straight lines. It is available in a wide range of fabric and leather upholstery in a choice of colors. The sofa rests on a shaker base in satin polished aluminum. The shell is made from a synthetic material and upholstered with cold-cured foam.

DESIGN: Arne Jacobsen
PRODUCER: Fritz Hansen A/S
YEAR OF DEVELOPMENT: 1958

Arne Jacobsen

DNA

The complex organic form of the DNA suspended lamp by Hopf & Wortmann has its origins in a very simple basic form. Pink, white, black or chrome plastic modules, each with three lightbulbs, combined in varying numbers to create a lamp of the desired size - from a single module to a voluminous chandelier. The individual modules are interchangeable and adjustable so each lamp can exist in many different forms and can be altered according to the wish or need of the moment. Its amorphous form makes the DNA lamp suitable for many interior contexts and is particularly eye-catching in pink. The designers at Büro für Form focus on creating product, interior and lighting design and accessories for renowned international manufacturers.

DESIGN: Hopf & Wortmann, Büro für Form
PRODUCER: next home collection e.K.
YEAR OF DEVELOPMENT: 2006
MAIN MATERIAL: ABS

Hopf & Wortmann,
Büro für Form

Block Table

Inspired by the well-known tray table, Danish designer Simon Legald designed Block as a light and airy mobile side table on wheels. The table is rectangular and is easy to move around using one of its four handles, which are a natural extension of the table's legs. Block is manufactured using steel and ash wood and is available in white, black, light gray, dark gray, mint green and coral, a warm and subtle shade of pink. It is easy to assemble and to clean. Simon Legald graduated from The Royal Danish Academy of Fine Arts in summer 2012. His work consists of both small-scale and large-scale products.

Simon Legald

DESIGN: Simon Legald
PRODUCER: Normann Copenhagen
YEAR OF DEVELOPMENT: 2012
MAIN MATERIAL: steel, ash wood

Elevated Vase

Designed by Thomas Bentzen for the Scandinavian company Muuto, this vase comprises a glass container elevated by a wooden bowl. Soft rose is one of three color options. The light glass vase is delicately mouth-blown and the solid ash bowl is crafted and shaped on a turning lathe. Functional, durable and simple, the design is representative of Thomas Bentzen's ethos. The designer started his own studio in 2010. He is co-designer of the design collective REMOVE and his products have received international recognition at fairs and exhibitions all over the world.

PHOTOS: COURTESY OF THE PRODUCER

Thomas Bentzen

DESIGN: Thomas Bentzen
PRODUCER: Muuto
YEAR OF DEVELOPMENT: 2013
MAIN MATERIAL: mouth-blown glass, solid ash wood

Mangas Space

Mangas Space comprises a range of multipurpose modules, cushions and poufs that can be combined and juxtaposed in any number of ways. Using a single set of items, the use and appearance of a space can be changed many times. All items are made of 100% virgin wool with cotton on the reverse. The cushions are filled with polyester and the poufs and modules with foam rubber. Colors available include ivory, yellow, coral and pink. The designer Patricia Urquiola was born in Spain and has lived and worked in Milan for more than 20 years. Her clients have included the Mandarin Oriental Hotel in Barcelona and the W Resort & Spa in Puerto Rico.

Patricia Urquiola

DESIGN: Patricia Urquiola
PRODUCER: GAN
YEAR OF DEVELOPMENT: 2013
MAIN MATERIAL: wool

Ro

Ro is an easy chair and footstool designed by Jaime Hayón for Fritz Hansen. It is available in nine unique design options with a mix of two fabrics, one for the shell and the second for the cushions. Ro is also available in a single fabric version and in leather. The legs are offered in brushed aluminum or oak. Jaime Hayón was born in Spain in 1974 and studied industrial design in Madrid and Paris. His first collections comprised designer toys, ceramics and furniture, later followed by interior design and installations. His work for Fritz Hansen includes the Ro easy chair and the FAVN sofa.

Jaime Hayon

DESIGN: Jaime Hayon
PRODUCER: Fritz Hansen A/S
YEAR OF DEVELOPMENT: 2013

Mhy Pendant Lamp

The Mhy Pendant Lamp was inspired by the illustrations and characters found in children's literature. It can be easily mounted in clusters or rows above a meeting table or in a canteen or reception. The lamp comprises a lacquered aluminum shade and a textile cord. The shade is made by a press and welded together. Each one is painted and assembled by hand. Norway Says is an internationally recognized design trio from Oslo which has received several prestigious prizes for their work including the Norwegian 'Designer of the Year' award. Other Muuto products by Norway Says include the Plus Salt and Pepper mills and the I'm Boo Carafe.

DESIGN: Norway Says
PRODUCER: Muuto
YEAR OF DEVELOPMENT: 2007
MAIN MATERIAL: aluminum wet painted socket in plastic, textile cord

Norway Says

Nerd Chair

The Nerd Chair by Muuto is simply designed and references classic Scandinavian design esthetics and values. Made of lacquered ash or oak wood, it is available in eight difference colors including rose, a soft finish that adds a feminine aspect to an otherwise stark design. The wood veneer is form-pressed into shape for the back and seat, before being glued together with the solid wood legs. Finally, the lacquer is applied. Designer David Geckeler studied industrial design in Berlin and Copenhagen. His chair design "Nerd" was honoured by Beckers International Design Award 2011 and is the winner of Muuto Talent Award 2011.

DESIGN: David Geckeler
PRODUCER: Muuto
YEAR OF DEVELOPMENT: 2012
MAIN MATERIAL: lacquered ash or oak wood, felt pads

David Geckeler

Folia Lumina

This set of LED lights was designed to resemble a plant, its leaves reflecting, discoloring, muting or strengthening the light. By clamping them onto the trunk and rotating or moving them, it is possible to instantly create new types of lighting and atmosphere. The Folia Lumina is made of porcelain, beechwood and paper and is available to purchase with a pink or green set of leaves.

The pink option creates a soft glowing light that is notable for its mellowing effects. Folia Lumina is one result of the collaboration between Dutch duo Tineke Beunders and Nathan Wierink. After studying together at the Design Academy in Eindhoven, they founded Ontwerpduo, now an established name in Dutch design.

DESIGN: Ontwerpduo
PRODUCER: Ontwerpduo
YEAR OF DEVELOPMENT: 2013
MAIN MATERIAL: paper leaves, ceramic pot, 3D-printed clamps

PHOTOS: COURTESY OF THE PRODUCER

Ontwerpduo

Kawa Collection

The Kawa Collection by Karim Rashid incorporates key bathroom components including a bath spout, single-lever washbasin, single-lever bidet mixer, shower column, shower holder, single-lever bath/shower mixer and concealed shower/bath panel. The collection is distinguished by the curved flat sections rounded on the ends that are featured in each item. Colors available include green and pink. Karim Rashid, a creative designer living in New York, has a thousand projects to his name for a range of different brands. He has received international recognition for his work.

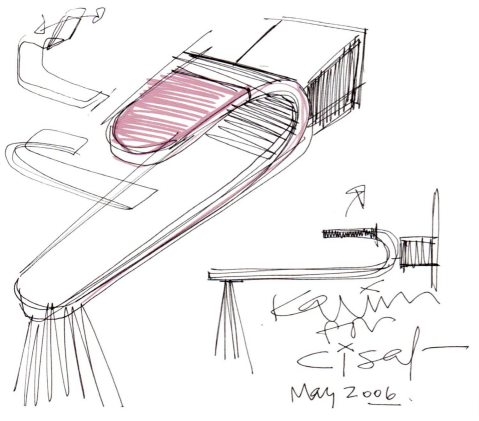

DESIGN: Karim Rashid
PRODUCER: Cisal
YEAR OF DEVELOPMENT: 2007
MAIN MATERIAL: powder-coated steel

PHOTOS: COURTESY OF KARIM RASHID, BANDO E&C CO., LTD. (PORTRAIT)

Karim Rashid

Dolomyth

Dolomyth aims to capture the complex relief of the Dolomites, which is rich in forms and the result of a successful and harmonious combination of structural shapes and climatic conditions. Alcarol retrieved blocks of local stone from an abandoned quarry. This stone is partially covered with native mosses and lichens giving it a surface that captures the geographical maps of the Dolomite's mountains. In the vertical section the different layers of geological sedimentation are clearly visible, with shades ranging from gray to antique pink, a soft and warm color. Alcarol has preserved the wrinkled natural surface of the rock by using a resin, freezing the present instant and endowing the blocks with new functionality and new design.

alcarol

DESIGN: alcarol
PRODUCER: alcarol
YEAR OF DEVELOPMENT: 2014
MAIN MATERIAL: dolomite rock with mosses and lichens, transparent resin, swivel casters

PHOTOS: COURTESY OF ALCAROL, ALBERTO BOGO (PORTRAIT)

Chaise A

During the 1930s, Xavier Pauchard, a metal worker from the Burgundy region, created the Tolix brand and went on to design a whole range of metal furniture, including the iconic Chaise A. This metal chair was to experience astonishing success: robust, stackable, it was used to fit out the desks of the steamship Normandie and, for more than 50 years, café terraces, village halls, hospitals and barracks. Given a facelift in 1986, it won over interior design professionals and the public, taking its place in the new art of living, and - the supreme accolade - achieved recognition among art historians. It remains a key component of any interior space and is now available in different pink scales.

DESIGN: Xavier Pauchard
PRODUCER: Tolix Steel Design
YEAR OF DEVELOPMENT: 1934
MAIN MATERIAL: steel

Echo Table

The Echo table by Debra Folz is a modern interpretation of the traditional patterns found in quilting. Each table consists of a welded base which holds four layers of glass. Each one-quarter inch layer of glass contributes one color or layer of the pattern. As the layers overlap, they create deeper hues and varying transparency. Space between the layers creates the impression that these layers are floating above one another. When natural light is introduced, the surface color and pattern are projected onto the floor beneath. The table is available in cerulean, smoke, violet and fuchsia, the last being a combination of darker and lighter shades of pink.

Debra Folz

DESIGN: Debra Folz
PRODUCER: Debra Folz Design
YEAR OF DEVELOPMENT: 2013
MAIN MATERIAL: steel, glass

PHOTOS: COURTESY OF THE PRODUCER

Kouple Bathtub

The Kouple bathtub for Korean company Saturn Bath is a two-person whirlpool bathtub with a joyous shape inspired by the form of two water drops. It is made from liquid acrylic and can be paired with the matching Kouple sink, both in designer Karim Rashid's signature color pink. This unusual bathroom furniture received the Red Dot Design Award in 2009. Rashid's designs are about the betterment of our lives in a poetic, esthetic, experiential, sensorial, and emotional way. His wish is to see people live in the modus of our time, to participate in the contemporary world, and to release themselves from nostalgia, antiquated traditions, old rituals and kitsch.

DESIGN: Karim Rashid
PRODUCER: Saturn Bath
YEAR OF DEVELOPMENT: 2008
MAIN MATERIAL: liquid acrylic

Karim Rashid

XXL Dome

This extra large fiberglass dome was designed by Ingo Maurer. The outer surface is the shade of aluminum silver while the matt interior can be lacquered in luminous orange, red, green or pink, the last of which is especially eye-catching. A key feature in a New York branch of the shoe chain Camper, the XXL Dome is an internationally successful design feature. Ingo Maurer began designing unique lamps and lighting systems in the 1960s and now manages a team of more than sixty in the company's Munich headquarters. Maurer's designs are displayed in a specially created showroom in the same city, the only one in Europe run by Ingo Maurer himself.

Ingo Maurer

DESIGN: Ingo Maurer
PRODUCER: Ingo Maurer GmbH
YEAR OF DEVELOPMENT: 1999
MAIN MATERIAL: fiberglass

PHOTOS: COURTESY OF THE PRODUCER

PANTONE Mugs

The PANTONE Mug is now an iconic product and recognized worldwide. Inspired by PANTONE's universal color charts, these bone china mugs are glazed with a color from PANTONE's color chip. The PANTONE name is known worldwide as the standard language for accurate color communication. The petal-like, blossom pink version is just one of a large range of colors available. The mug is dishwasher and microwave safe. Jackie Piper and Victoria Whitbread's company 'Designed in Colour' has its showroom and studio in the London Oxo Tower.

Jackie Piper, Victoria Whitbread

DESIGN: Jackie Piper, Victoria Whitbread
PRODUCER: Whitbread Wilkinson
YEAR OF DEVELOPMENT: 2007
MAIN MATERIAL: high-quality white light bone China

Pushboy Classic Line

The key features of the Pushboy Classic Line by Wesco include its fixed base, stable metal handles and decorative embossing. Rubbish is pushed through the large stainless steel flap which also prevents any unpleasant aromas escaping from the bin. The Pushboy is made out of powder-coated steel plates, ensuring stability and durability. Beneath the decorative exterior, the metal insert has a volume of 50 liters. The bin shares its rounded form, combination of materials and colorful exterior with several other products in the Wesco range. Available colors include red, orange, black, almond, white and pink.

PRODUCER: Wesco
YEAR OF DEVELOPMENT: 2006
MAIN MATERIAL: powder-coated sheet steel, stainless steel

Miss Dior Chair

The Miss Dior Chair is part of a 'Room Of One's Own' writing pavilion by Slovenian designer Nika Zupanc. She used Virginia Woolf's essay as inspiration for the small, latticed pavilion complete with table, chair and lamp. Miss Dior motifs, such as the bow and the pale pink color, were incorporated into the chair's design. A scaled-down version of the cane work was used for the seat. Zupanc was one of fifteen designers asked by curator Herve Mikaeloff to contribute to a 2013 exhibition celebrating the Miss Dior perfume. The pavilion was on display in the Galerie Courbe at the Grand Palais in Paris.

DESIGN: Nika Zupanc
PRODUCER: Dior
YEAR OF DEVELOPMENT: 2012
MAIN MATERIAL: metal tube, wood

Nika Zupanc

FAVN

The FAVN sofa was designed by Jaime Hayon for Fritz Hansen in 2011. FAVN, the Danish word for 'embrace', is the result of a creative dialogue between the Spanish designer, Jaime Hayon and Fritz Hansen. The sofa is available in nine unique options comprising a mix of three fabrics; one fabric for the shell, one for the seat and back cushions, and the third for the small decorative cushions. The sofa is also available in a single fabric version. There are several color options including gray, black, yellow and light pink. The range of accessories includes loose decorative cushions and large felt glides for soft floors.

DESIGN: Jaime Hayon
PRODUCER: Fritz Hansen A/S
YEAR OF DEVELOPMENT: 2011

Jaime Hayon

KitchenAid Artisan Stand Mixer and Artisan Blender

The Artisan Stand Mixer with its patented planetary paddle mixer has featured in KitchenAid's product list for many years. One version is exhibited in the Museum of Modern Art in New York. It is notable for its wide range of functions, its durability and its range of colors. The mixer is made entirely from metal. There are a wide range of optional accessories that can be fitted to the mixer through the single attachment hub. The Artisan Blender has a solid, American design. The 1.5 liter container is made from shatter-proof glass while the colored base is manufactured from injection molded metal. The iconic Stand Mixer was born in 1919. And from that stemmed an entire range of high-performance appliances - all created with the same attention to detail, quality craftsmanship, versatile technology and timeless design.

PRODUCER: KitchenAid
YEAR OF DEVELOPMENT: 1919
MAIN MATERIAL: zinc die-cast/molded metal

CH05 THIS

The apparently simple chair exemplifies the basic principles of e15, who seek to expose and emphasize a product's essential elements in its design. Named after the famous card trick, the series of chairs THIS THAT OTHER is constructed from robust and versatile plywood with an oak veneer. Contemporary elements combine with round forms, rational details and high-quality materials and manufacture. Due to its efficient construction, the chair THIS is designed as a particularly economical option for consumers. The neon pink version was developed by e15 art director Farah Ebrahimi and is one of several colors available. The chair can be purchased with or without an upholstered seat.

DESIGN: Stefan Diez
PRODUCER: e15 Design und Distributions GmbH
YEAR OF DEVELOPMENT: 2013
MAIN MATERIAL: oak-veneered plywood, clear or color-lacquered

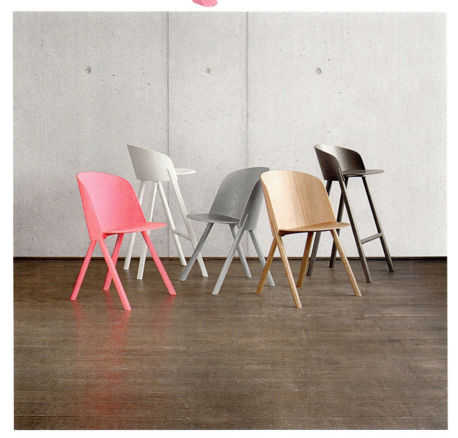

Stefan Diez

Beater Whisk

The German design trio Ding3000 has created this space-saving functional whisk that can be folded together for compact storage in the kitchen drawer or on the wall. Beater is inspired by a pack of straws and is gathered in the middle using a ring that functions as both an opening and closing mechanism and a hanging fixture. Navy blue, gray, nude and pink are just some of the eight colors available. It is manufactured from nylon and is suitable for the dishwasher. Ding3000 have won several awards for their design, including the Red Dot Design Award 2012 and DesignPlus 2013 in Germany.

DESIGN: Ding3000
PRODUCER: Normann Copenhagen
YEAR OF DEVELOPMENT: 2012
MAIN MATERIAL: nylon

Kitchen Scales

The Bloomingville line of scales has been developed with great emphasis on reviving an iconic vintage kitchen tool and enhancing it with new colors. The scale has been a common kitchen tool from the beginning of the 20th century, originally designed for horizontal surfaces. Putting the goods in the tin pan on top would force the spring down and show the weight to the user on the large front dial. Although digital scales have replaced spring scales in many modern kitchens, the esthetic of the older design is still in demand. The trendy pink color adds a contemporary note to this classic design. Made of durable painted metal with a stainless steel bowl, the Bloomingville scale is available in two sizes and measures up to 3kg or 5kg in increments of 10g.

DESIGN: Betina Stampe
PRODUCER: Bloomingville
YEAR OF DEVELOPMENT: 2014
MAIN MATERIAL: metal

Betina Stampe

RTY DAR

Chopping Board

This large chopping board with neon pink edge is made from acacia wood and is one of many products for the kitchen designed and made by RICE. RICE is a Danish manufacturer of articles and accessories for the home, including colorful melamine products, handmade baskets and containers and handmade ceramics from Portugal. Inspired by "the good old days", the designers seek to create colorful products that will make their users feel at home. All of their products that are involved in food preparation undergo stringent testing in order that the highest safety standards might be maintained.

Charlotte Hedeman Gueniau

DESIGN: Charlotte Hedeman Gueniau
PRODUCER: RICE
YEAR OF DEVELOPMENT: 2014
MAIN MATERIAL: acacia wood

Paperfold

The Paperfold lamp series by Kjellgren Kaminsky Architecture was inspired by colorful paper and beautiful collars. The unusual forms were developed through experimenting with the possibilities of paper as a design tool. Each of the lamps in the Paperfold series derives from the same idea and carries echoes of its siblings in its design. The lamps are availbale in four different colors: black, cyan, amber and magenta, the last of which is particularly striking. Kjellgren Kaminsky Architecture are based in Gothenburg and seek sustainable solutions in all of their architectural and design projects.

Fredrik Kjellgren

PHOTOS: COURTESY OF KJELLGREN KAMINSKY ARCHITECTURE

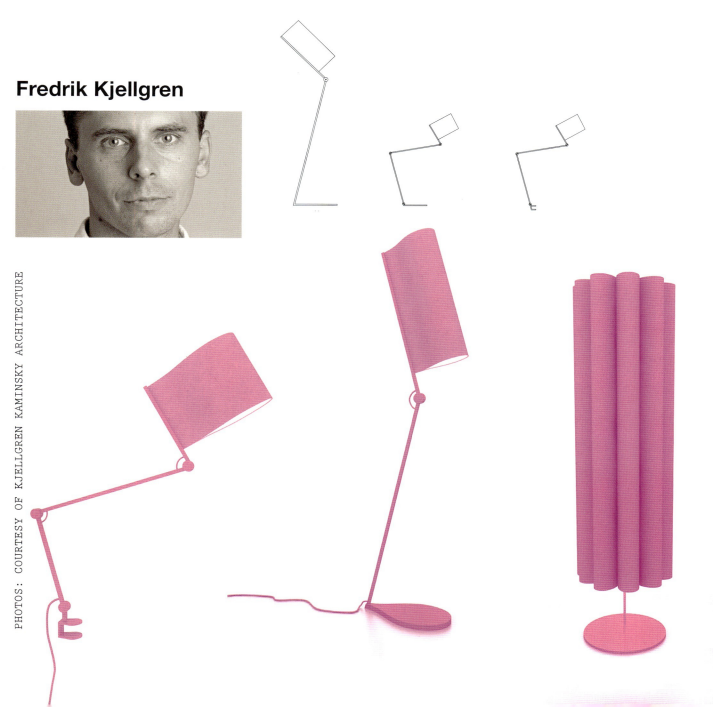

Series 7

Sixty years ago, Arne Jacobsen designed the Series 7 chair, earning himself and Republic of Fritz Hansen a prominent place in design history. The 3107 is its latest incarnation. Designed to be solid and durable, the chair is made of pressure molded sliced veneer and chromed steel tubes. Ten different veneers are available, including maple, beech, ash and cherry, as well as an ash or lacquer finish in a variety of colors. Front or full upholstery is available in a wide range of fabrics and leathers. Two special anniversary limited editions of the 3107 chair have been made, one in dark blue and the second in pale pink with 24 carat gold-plated legs.

DESIGN: Arne Jacobsen
PRODUCER: Fritz Hansen A/S
YEAR OF DEVELOPMENT: 1955
MAIN MATERIAL SHELL: pressure-molded veneer

Arne Jacobsen

popstahl kitchen

This kitchen by popstahl is made from 100% steel, making it robust and durable. The color is applied through a process of powder coating in which no solvents are used and the color is fused directly with the metal. Over 100 RAL colors are available, including this vibrant red beet option. New colors can be layered on top of the old one to create new looks and individual parts exchanged for others in a different color. The purpose-built colored paneling on the face fits flush with the steel sheets and contrasts with the metal. Popstahl's kitchens can be 100% recycled, although the durability of the materials means that replacement is rare.

DESIGN: architects Christian Thommes and Ralf Weissheimer
PRODUCER: popstahl Thommes and Weissheimer
YEAR OF DEVELOPMENT: 2009
MAIN MATERIAL: powder-coated galvanized sheet steel

Christian Thommes, Ralf Weissheimer

Chestnut Lamp

The Chestnut paper origami lampshade is designed to have an angular exterior and a curved interior shape. It is folded with the utmost precision from one piece of FSC paper. It is available in several colors including canary yellow, autumn green, gray, white and pink, while the textile cord can be purchased in red, blue, gray, yellow, black, white or pink. The lampshade fits around a standard energy-saving light bulb and is suitable for use in a dining room, lounge or bedroom. Studio Snowpuppe is based in The Hague and comprises three paper engineers, Nellianna, Kenneth and Fleur, who create the folded paper lamps.

DESIGN: Nellianna van den Baard, Kenneth Veenenbos
PRODUCER: Studio Snowpuppe
YEAR OF DEVELOPMENT: 2010
MAIN MATERIAL: paper

Kenneth Veenenbos, Nellianna van den Baard

PHOTOS : COURTESY OF THE PRODUCER

Smoke Alarms

The Kupu and Lento smoke detectors were designed according to the principle that a good smoke alarm is not hidden but should be a feature of the home. The aim was to encourage all householders to include and display this essential item as part of their furnishings. Two Finnish designers, Harri Koskinen and Paola Suhonen, were chosen to create the smoke alarm. The former is known for his timeless and innovative designs and the latter for her refreshing style and her "rock chick" outlook. The Kupu is available in white, brown, green, gray, chrome or pink and can be installed in seconds. There is no single button, but rather the whole surface functions as the switch.

DESIGN: Harri Koskinen (Kupu),
Paola Suhonen (Lento)
PRODUCER: Jalo Helsinki

PHOTOS: COURTESY OF THE PRODUCER

SIGG Bottles

The Original Bottle by SIGG is molded from a piece of pure aluminum in a Swiss factory in Frauenfeld. It is intended for use on a range of excursions including hikes or bike trips. It features a leakproof fastening that ensures no drop of liquid can escape. All SIGG bottles are 100% recyclable and are known for their high quality and ease of use. They are also breakproof and suitable for use by children. Several SIGG bottles are available in various shades of pink, including the 0.75 liter WMB Sports Pink Touch, the 0.3 liter Farmyard Family and the 0.6 liter in fabulous pink. SIGG was founded in Switzerland in 1908 and is now known worldwide for its reusable aluminum bottles.

PRODUCER: SIGG
YEAR OF DEVELOPMENT: 2014
MAIN MATERIAL: aluminum

PANTONE Coffee Maker

The PANTONE Coffee Maker by Jackie Piper and Victoria Whitbread of 'Designed in Colour' was inspired by a classic percolating coffee maker design and updated with vibrant colors. Hot Pink 215 is just one of several colors available. The coffee maker can be mixed and matched with PANTONE espresso cups or mugs. Victoria and Jackie founded the company in 2001 as a creative hub offering contemporary and colorful design-led products. Creators of the now iconic PANTONE mug and other award-winning products and ranges, 'Designed in Colour' are seeking to build their portfolio of high-quality homewares and gift for the consumer.

Jackie Piper, Victoria Whitbread

DESIGN: Jackie Piper, Victoria Whitbread
PRODUCER: Whitbread Wilkinson
YEAR OF DEVELOPMENT: 2013
MAIN MATERIAL: aluminum

Willydilly Bon

The Ingo Maurer classic Willydilly from 1983 is now available in luminous orange and pink. Willydilly Bon is a new variation of the hanging lamp that Maurer created in 1983. Now, as then, the outer surface is made of translucent white cardboard, while the reverse now features a neon orange or pink surface. Different lightbulbs produce varying effects: a conventional bulb will radiate upwards and downwards and illuminate the colored shade almost completely while a retrofit LED bulb will shine mostly downwards and only partially illuminate the shade, generating a less intense effect. The pink shade creates a particularly striking and compelling light.

Ingo Maurer

DESIGN: Ingo Maurer
PRODUCER: Ingo Maurer GmbH
YEAR OF DEVELOPMENT: 1983/2014
MAIN MATERIAL: cardboard, plastic, wire

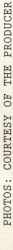

Sebastiano Pen Holder

The Sebastiano pen holder is made of thermoplastic resin and contains twenty holes for storing pens and other writing tools. It was designed by Massimo Giacon and its unique face resembles the same designer's Mr. Suicide bath plug. The pen holder is available in black, green and pink. Massimo Giacon is just one of many designers who have created items for Alessi, all of whose products are the result of long-standing collaboration with the best international designers. They aim to create a broad range of accessible products suitable for every home with a strong emphasis on high quality and uniqueness.

DESIGN: LPWK - Massimo Giacon
PRODUCER: Alessi
YEAR OF DEVELOPMENT: 2004
MAIN MATERIAL: thermoplastic resin

LAMY safari

Designed for young people, the LAMY safari fountain pen combines a classic design with ergonomic comfort. The first LAMY safari appeared on the market in 1980 and was popular amongst pupils. The pen is now available in a broad range of colors and special editions, including a striking shade of bright pink. It has turned into a stylish accessory not only at school but for all generations. It is made of sturdy plastic and features a steel nib and metal clip. Several accessories are available including a piston operated converter and the LAMY giant ink cartridge. An independent family business, Lamy was founded in 1930 by C. Josef Lamy. In 1966, the distinctive product form by Lamy, the Lamy Design, was born through the LAMY 2000.

DESIGN: Wolfgang Fabian/C. Josef Lamy GmbH
PRODUCER: C. Josef Lamy GmbH
YEAR OF DEVELOPMENT: 1980
MAIN MATERIAL: ABS-plastic

Moleskine Colored Notebooks

The Moleskine notebook is the successor to the legendary notebooks used by artists and thinkers over the past two centuries. In the mid-1980s the notebook that Bruce Chatwin nicknamed "moleskine" became increasingly scarce and then disappeared completely. In 1997, a small Milanese publisher brought the famous notebook back to life and expanded the Moleskine range to encompass an array of nomadic objects including bags, apps and writing instruments as well as notebooks. These colored notebook versions are thread-bound and feature rounded corners, acid-free paper, a bookmark ribbon, elastic closure and an expandable inner pocket. The vibrant pink option adds a trendy twist to the timeless design.

PRODUCER: Moleskine
YEAR OF DEVELOPMENT: 2011-2014
MAIN MATERIAL: coated cardboard, paper

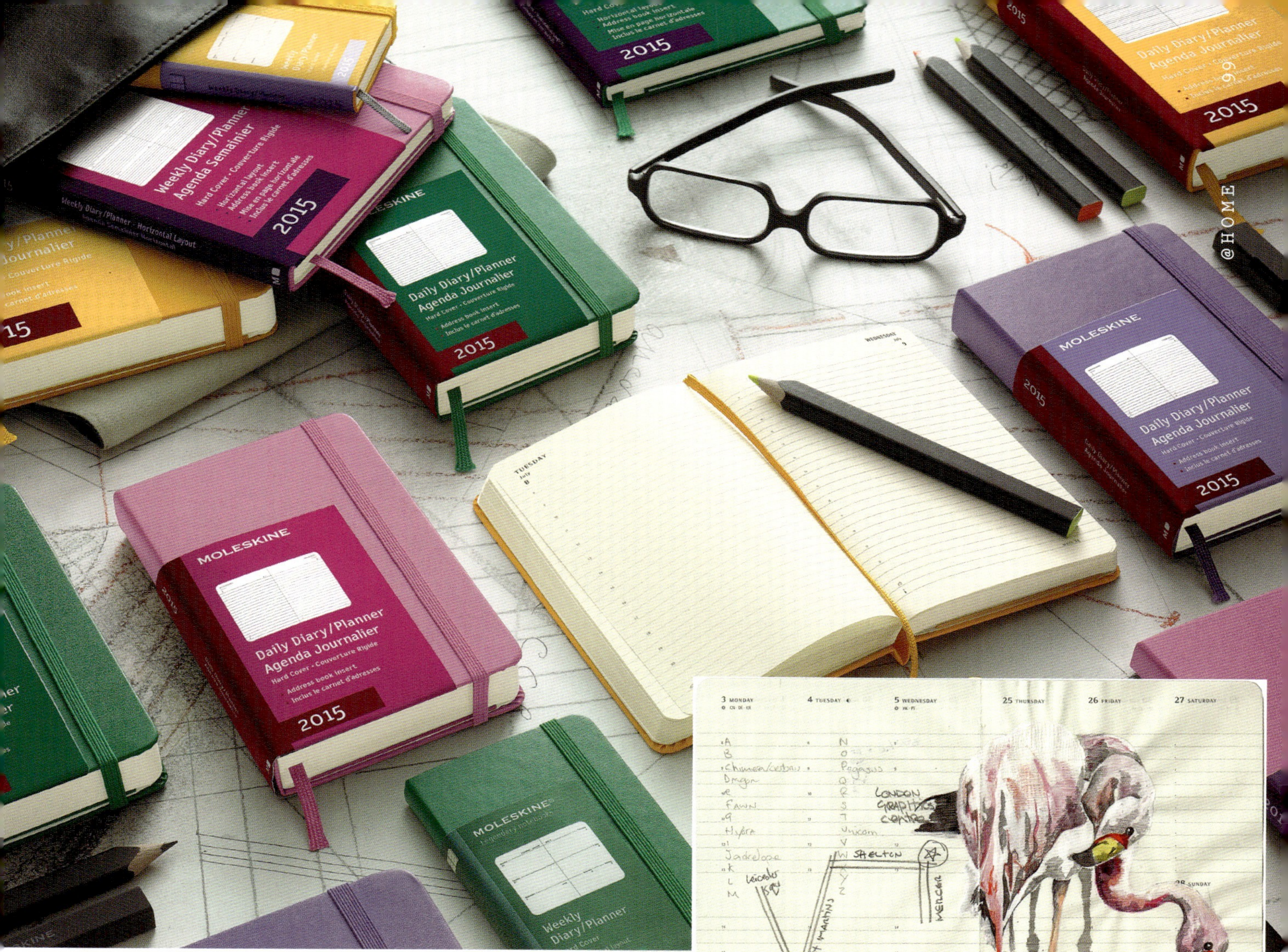

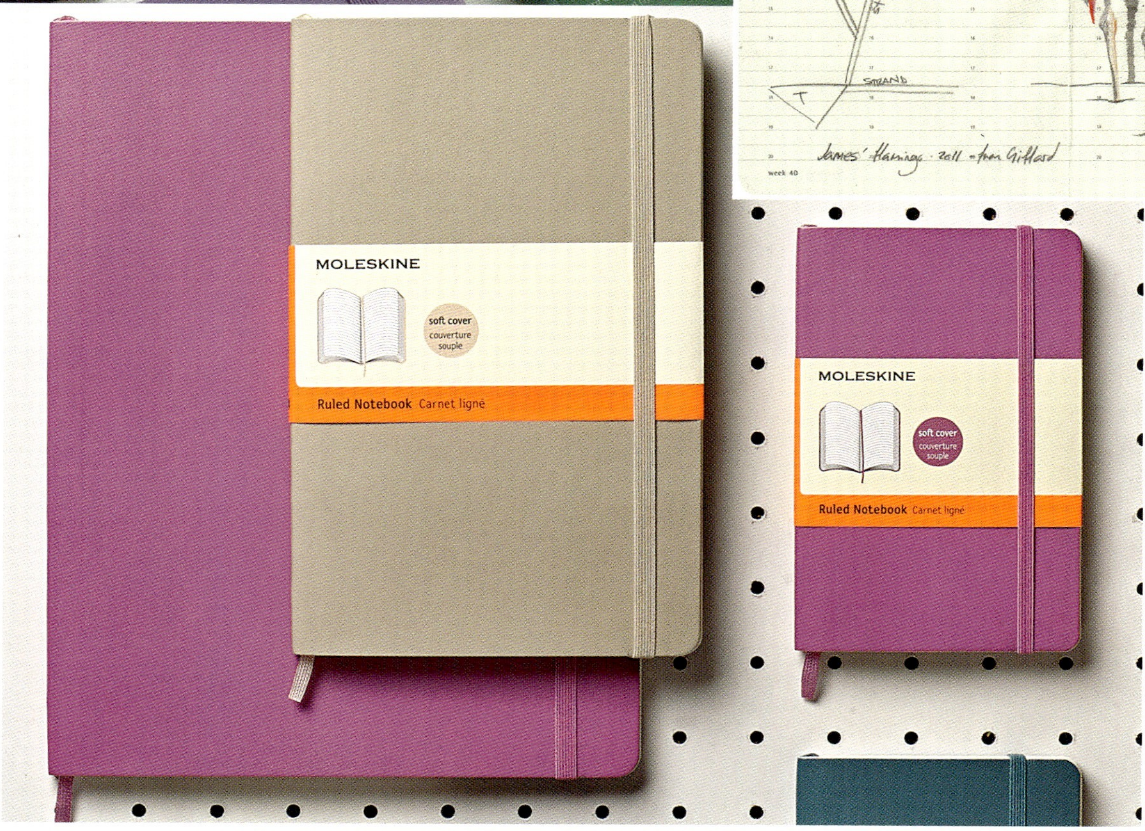

PHOTOS: COURTESY OF THE PRODUCER

FASHION & ACCESSORIES

Pure

In 2013, Ruco Line, a company specializing in the manufacture of high-quality designer sneakers, began a project of international appeal to create partnerships with prominent figures from various sectors including art, music, sport and lifestyle. A collaboration between Daniela Penchini of Ruco Line and French architect Jean Nouvel led to the creation of the Pure sneaker.

Previewed at the Milan International Furniture Fair 2013, Pure has since then been distributed via Ruco Line's sales channels, elite boutiques throughout the world and via Gagosian channels on the occasion of the special cooperation with the Art Gallery. It is available not only in several colors including black, white and pink, but also in different materials according to the season.

DESIGN: Jean Nouvel Studio
PRODUCER: Ruco Line
YEAR OF DEVELOPMENT: 2013
MAIN MATERIAL: upper lining: smooth, greased calf leather; lining: calf leather, rubber sole

836
NVL PR 13   37#FX 06 2013

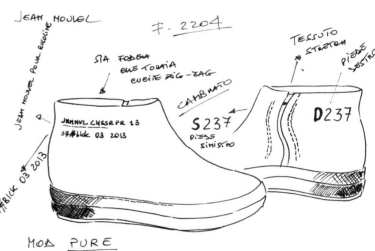

Jean Nouvel Studio

Ice-Watch

The unique design of the brand Ice-Watch is reflected in the models and colors which are available in over 400 different combinations. For every taste, every style and every situation there is a suitable Ice-Watch model. Founded in Belgium in 2007, Ice-Watch watches are sold in over 85 countries. The Belgian headquarters is the focal point of all the ideas and creativity - and of course the guide for all economic and conceptual approaches. The founder Jean-Pierre Lutgen strongly focuses on the concept and the spirit behind the brand.

PRODUCER: Ice-Watch
YEAR OF DEVELOPMENT: 2007
MAIN MATERIAL: silicone

4711 ACQUA COLONIA
Pink Pepper & Grapefruit

ACQUA COLONIA from the House of 4711 is a series of fragrances comprising natural ingredients chosen to have a positive effect on the user's mood. The Pink Pepper & Grapefruit version is offered in a bright pink container that is intended to signify vibrancy and gleefulness. The flask and folding box feature a retro design, while the 170ml version is offered in a traditional Molanus bottle with a high-quality finish. In a subtle shade of green, the box depicts individual ingredients in a series of stylish botanical drawings. The label describes the fragrance in six different languages. Cécile Hua, perfumer and creator of this scent, is a passionate globetrotter and winner of the renowned Fashion Group International Rising Star Award.

DESIGN: peter schmidt, belliero & zandée
PRODUCER: 4711
YEAR OF DEVELOPMENT: 2013

Pink Lace Choker

The Lace choker by Saskia Diez is a five strand neckpiece available in black, turquoise, nude or pink. The beads are made of lacquered wood from local maple and beech trees and are threaded onto elastic nylon. A silver clasp at the back is made of sterling silver. This choker is one of many jewelry pieces designed by Saskia Diez for her own label. She works closely with goldsmiths and other craftspeople in and around Munich and sources many of her materials locally. The products are also manufactured in Munich, while the gold and silver used in her designs are mainly from recycled materials.

DESIGN: Saskia Diez
PRODUCER: Saskia Diez
YEAR OF DEVELOPMENT: 2013
MAIN MATERIAL: wood, lacquer, sterling silver

Saskia Diez

PHOTOS: BENJAMIN LINDENKREUZ, ATELIER SASKIA DIEZ (STILL),
JULIAN BAUMANN (PORTRAIT)

Chuck Taylor All Star

The Chuck Taylor All Star in pink is a classic Converse design in a modern color. They feature a thick rubber sole and a canvas upper. Converse is a cult American designer of sportswear and sneakers based in Massachusetts. It was founded in 1908 by Marquis M. Converse who manufactured winter shoes under the name Converse Rubber Shoe Company. In 1917, the now globally renowned All Star, also known as Chucks, came on the market featuring the signature of basketball star Chuck Taylor. Since then, 600 million pairs of All Stars have been sold worldwide and become renowned for their sportiness and trendiness.

PRODUCER: Converse
YEAR OF DEVELOPMENT: 1917
MAIN MATERIAL: rubber sole, canvas upper

Acer x Christian Cowan-Sanluis Selfie Hat

In September 2014, during the London Fashion Week, Acer announced its unique collaboration with fashion designer Christian Cowan-Sanluis. The hat comes in a sparkly pink design and is enhanced with Acer's advanced technology from the Tab 8 tablet, which helps detect the user's best angles whilst the selfie camera is activated, letting them snap and review photos from any angle desired. Users can also access other apps such as Facebook and Instagram whilst wearing the hat. As part of the collaboration, Acer and Christian Cowan-Sanluis have also created ten limited edition pink sparkly glitter cases with accompanying hats in the same style as the selfie hat.

DESIGN: Acer x Christian Cowan-Sanluis
YEAR OF DEVELOPMENT: 2014
MAIN MATERIAL: glitter canvas, steel strips and plastic corrugated card

Christian Cowan-Sanluis

Rib'N'Rope

The necklace Rib'N'Rope was inspired by minimalist design. The partially flattened stainless steel elements mark the transition from flat grosgrain ribbon to chunky sailing rope and from various shades of pink to signal red. Several hues of pink are incorporated into different versions of the necklace, from soft rose to vibrant fuchsia.

Heike Walk's designs are influenced by the observation of everyday objects, events and stories. Tiny details are used as inspiration for pieces of jewelry that resonate with the essential elements of everyday items. Heike Walk is based in Cologne, Germany.

DESIGN: Heike Walk
PRODUCER: Heike Walk
YEAR OF DEVELOPMENT: 2014
MAIN MATERIAL: stainless steel, ribbon nautical rope, cotton yarn

Heike Walk

adidas ZX8000 Bravo "Fall of the Wall"

For the 25th anniversary of the fall of the Berlin Wall, Adidas Originals pays tribute to the most important event of recent German history with its classic ZX8000 range. It comes in three different color combinations, each based on one of the wall's military checkpoints, Alpha, Bravo and Charlie. The ZX8000 Bravo is the most colorful and resembles the Checkpoint Bravo building in Drewitz-Dreilinden. In pink nubuck, the shoe features synthetic underlays, a bright yellow heel cage and light blue elements on the midsole. The "Made in Germany" models in premium suede, nubuck and leather were manufactured in the last remaining sneaker factory in Germany and were released on 8th November 2014.

PRODUCER: adidas
YEAR OF DEVELOPMENT: 2014
MAIN MATERIAL: nubuck

Triangl Bikinis

Triangl was founded in 2012 by duo Craig Ellis and Erin Deering. From a casual chat on a beach in Melbourne, they decided there was a gap in the market for affordable designer swimwear. They founded Triangl not long afterwards. Traingl bikinis are all designed and produced in Neoprene, a fabric known for its smoothing and supportive properties. The bikinis are bright and bold with a focus on block color combinations. Working with an extensive color palette, their designs range from pretty pastels to bright neon colors.

Craig Ellis, Erin Deering

DESIGN: Triangl
PRODUCER: Triangl
YEAR OF DEVELOPMENT: 2012
MAIN MATERIAL: neoprene

TOMS Classics

In 2006, American traveler Blake Mycoskie befriended children in a village in Argentina and found they had no shoes to protect their feet. Wanting to help, he created TOMS, a company that would match every pair of shoes purchased with a pair of new shoes given to a child in need. Realizing that One for One® could serve other global needs,

Blake has since launched TOMS Eyewear to help restore sight to persons in need and a bag collection to help provide safe births to mothers and babies. The TOMS shoe collection incorporates many designs available for women, men and children in pink, from wellies to canvas, plaid or glittery classics.

PRODUCER: TOMS
YEAR OF DEVELOPMENT: 2006
MAIN MATERIAL: canvas, elastic V, suede insole, mix-rubber outsole

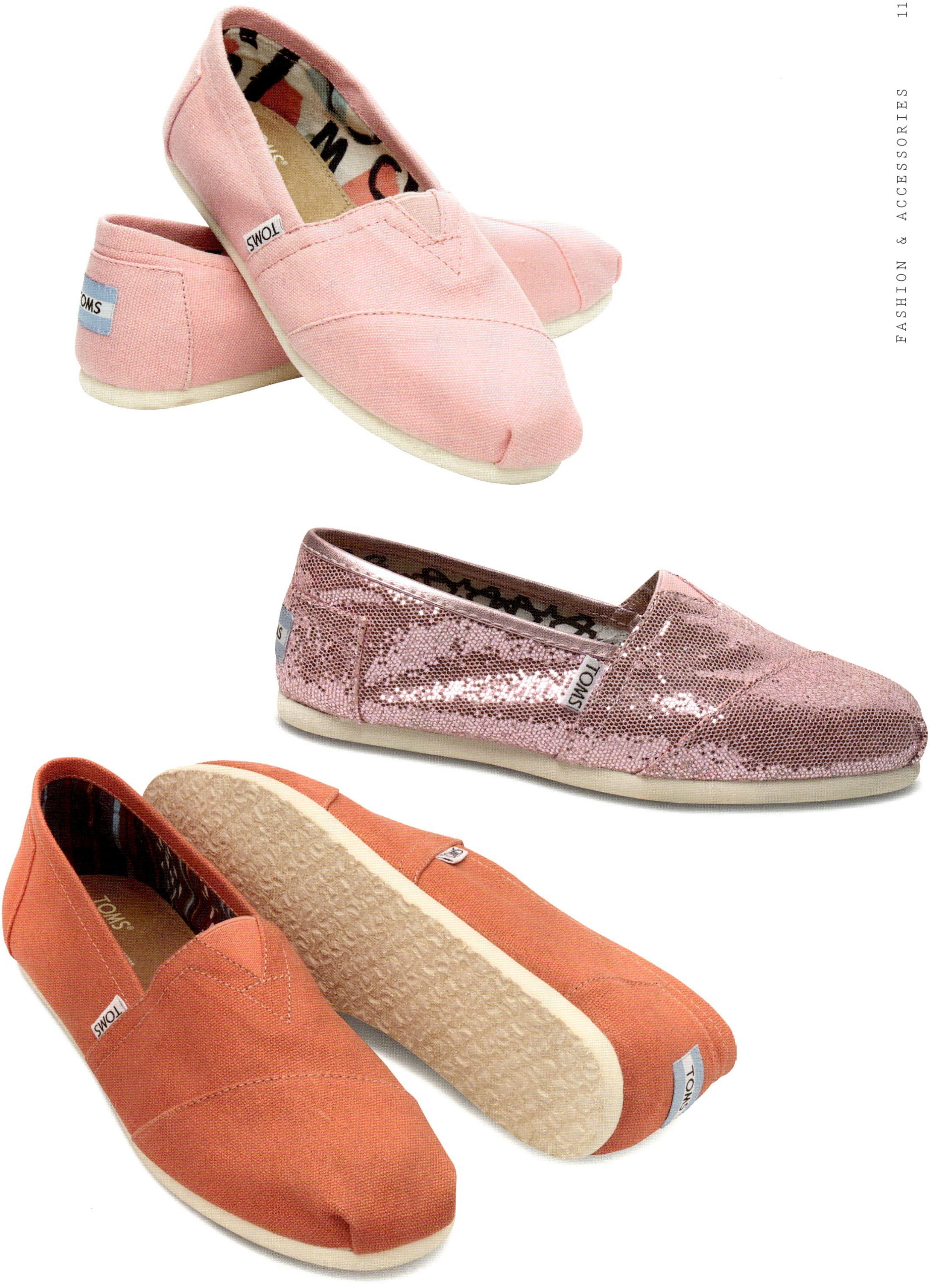

PHOTOS: COURTESY OF THE PRODUCER

Tote Bags

This tote bag is handmade from natural dyed linen with a gradient. It features long natural leather handles, a removable leather zip wallet and a linen lining. The leather is natural cow leather, vegetal tanned. The bag is hand-painted with eco-textile colors based on mineral pigments. Designer Margarete Häusler studied textile and surface design at a Berlin art school before working with ceramics and later textiles. She lived in Paris for several years, working as a designer, stylist and photographer, before creating her own label in 2009. She is based in Berlin.

DESIGN: Margarete Häusler
PRODUCER: Margarete Häusler
YEAR OF DEVELOPMENT: 2014
MAIN MATERIAL: dyed linen, leather

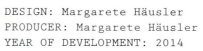

JOOP! Homme

The JOOP! Homme fragrance is available as eau de toilette, shower gel, mild deodorant spray and after-shave, all in pink packaging. First created in 1989, the fragrance has been available ever since. The scent is flowery, woody and oriental, combining the cool freshness of bergamot with heart notes of cinnamon and top notes of orange blossom. Hints of sandalwood, vetiver and patchouli, as well as amber, tobacco and a whiff of honey are also present. JOOP! was founded in 1986 by German fashion designer Wolfgang Joop. The brand offers contemporary menswear and womenswear as well as watches, jewelry and fragrances.

PRODUCER: COTY
YEAR OF DEVELOPMENT: 1989

Chopard Happy Sport Medium Automatic

The Happy Sport Medium Automatic in rose gold by Chopard has a guilloché silver dial. Seven diamonds move between the sapphire glasses. It has a diameter of 36 millimeters and is attached to the wearer's wrist with a strap either made of alligator leather or satin. The mechanical movement of the watch can be viewed through the back of the case. The watch is self-winding and is water resistant up to 30 meters. Roman numerals feature on the dial along with the date at the 4 o'clock position. Chopard is a high-end watch and jewelry company founded in 1860 and based in Switzerland.

PRODUCER: CHOPARD
YEAR OF DEVELOPMENT: 2014
MAIN MATERIAL: rose gold, diamonds, satin

PHOTOS: COURTESY OF THE PRODUCER

KENZO Jeu d'Amour

The feminine scent of KENZO's Amour range features top notes of pomegranate, tea and mandarin orange and heart notes of tuberose (a night-blooming plant with waxy white flowers) and freesia. A sensual base comprises hints of milky sandalwood and white musk. The bottle and packaging were designed by Karim Rashid, who used soft pink tones and an image of red lips to create a suitable counterpart to the fragrance. KENZO was founded in Paris in 1970 by Japanese designer Kenzo Takada. Beginning with handmade women's clothing, he later branched out into menswear, childrenswear and home collections. Today, KENZO is an international luxury goods brand that offers clothing, accessories and, through its sister company KENZO Parfums, fragrances.

Karim Rashid

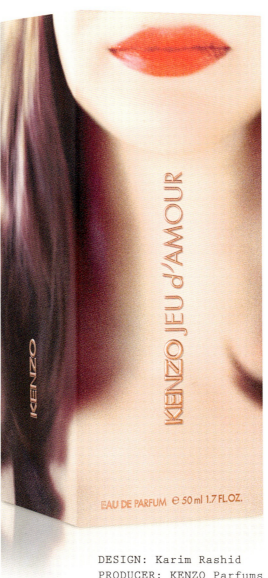

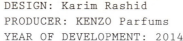

PHOTOS: COURTESY OF THE PRODUCER, MILOVAN KNEZEVIC (PORTRAIT)

DESIGN: Karim Rashid
PRODUCER: KENZO Parfums
YEAR OF DEVELOPMENT: 2014

TRANSPORTATION

FlyingBike

The FlyingBike saddle cover by Donkey is intended as a stylish and humorous addition to a functional item. It is available in silver, neon yellow or pink, the last of which is a bright but warm hue. The high-visibility, reflective wings enhance the rider's safety by ensuring he or she is clearly visible to other road users. The saddle cover is made of 100% polyester and measures 28 x 25 centimeters. It is one of many novelty items offered by Donkey who design and produce fun everyday products for the kitchen, bathroom, office and living spaces as well as products to accessorize an outdoor lifestyle.

PRODUCER: Donkey Products
YEAR OF DEVELOPMENT: 2014
MAIN MATERIAL: polyester

CUBE Sting WLS SL 29

This CUBE bike for women is designed to be sporty and dynamic yet feminine. There are no conventionally girly details but rather vibrant hues of pink and purple in combination with black. The smallest frame size is 13.5 inches and comes with 27.5 inch wheels to achieve the optimum mix of geometry, riding position, kinematics and the fast-rolling characteristics of bigger wheels. The triple butted aluminum frame has a lowered top tube for more standover clearance. Suspension components include a Fox Float CTD shock with adjustable rebound and CUBE custom tune and the lightweight Fox 32 Float CTD fork.

DESIGN: Carolin Lippert
PRODUCER: CUBE
YEAR OF DEVELOPMENT: 2013
MAIN MATERIAL: aluminum

Carolin Lippert

GLOBE Skateboards

GLOBE is a French firm whose products include casual clothing, accessories, shoes and skateboards. The Bantam Clear in watermelon, a vivid shade of pink, has a clear color-tinted deck, wide trucks and a steep kick tail. The design is inspired by 1960s and 1970s plastic skateboards, to which modern,

fully functional performance aspects have been added. The Blazer in blazing pink has a color dipped, stained 7-ply maple deck with laser-etched logo, wheel wells knocking back to wood and assorted printed griptape. Inspired by the Bantam, the Blazer features all the same components.

PRODUCER: GLOBE
YEAR OF DEVELOPMENT: 2014
MAIN MATERIAL: heavy-duty plastic (Bantam
Clear), resin-7 hard rock maple (Blazer)

Cinelli Vigorelli

The Cinelli Vigorelli is a cult track bike available in pink. It is manufactured from Columbus Airplane aluminum tubing (triple butted) and features Columbus Pista carbon forks. Its semislope geometry makes it reactive, agile and sharp. A new conical seat tube with a conical shape enables increased pedaling efficiency. The Vigorelli bike is used by the Cinelli Chrome Team and is often seen in races such as the famous Red Hood Criterium held in Brooklyn, Barcelona and Milan. The words "ellisse magica" (ellipse magic) inscribed on the seat tube refer to the historical name of the legendary Milanese Velodrome, renowned for track cycling.

DESIGN: Alessandra Cusatelli, R&D Cinelli dpt
PRODUCER: Cinelli
YEAR OF DEVELOPMENT: 2012
MAIN MATERIAL: aluminum, carbon fiber

Alessandra Cusatelli

Honda SH Mode 125

The SH Mode 125 was launched in 2014 and is available in pearl fabulous pink, poseidon black metallic and pearl jasmine white. It has a lightweight, compact body, a responsive, fuel injected engine, Idle Stop as standard and Honda's Combined Braking System (CBS). Its low seat and spacious floor were designed to make the riding experience as comfortable as possible. A large secure storage area in the seat has enough space for a full face helmet or other essential items. The premium instrument panel providing all necessary information, as well as the tail light and the sculpted headlights have all been styled with the aim of creating a chic and elegant bike for women.

PRODUCER: Honda
YEAR OF DEVELOPMENT: 2012

Harley-Davidson Forty-Eight Custombike

Like all Harley models, the Forty-Eight is easily customized to suit the owner's taste. Its features include a fat MT90 front wheel in custom rubber, a slammed drag-style handlebar with speedometer and under mount mirrors and a rear end with retro-styled Stop-Turn-Tail lights. The lowered front and rear suspension and a low solo seat ensure a responsive ride. The bike also features the traditional 2.1 gallon (7.95 liter) peanut fuel tank. Customized features on this model include the pink-painted fuel tank, the ornamental pink rings on the tires, the engine cover decorated with rhinestones and the modified exhaust system in black.

DESIGN: Motomaxx
PRODUCER: Harley-Davidson
YEAR OF DEVELOPMENT: 2011
MAIN MATERIAL: steel

Electra Bikes

The Cruiser was the bike that launched Electra twenty-two years ago. Adapted from an American classic, the frame geometry was opened up, the pedals moved forward, the seat angle relaxed and the body given more breathing room. It also features Electra's patented Flat Foot Technology®. Customers can now choose between an alloy or steel frame, single or multiple gears and a variety of styles and accessories. The Amsterdam is a modern take on the Dutch city bike. It features fast-rolling 700c wheels, Flat Foot Technology®, a full chainguard and fenders. Pink is one of several colors in which these bikes are available. Electra Bicycle Company is the leading lifestyle bicycle brand in the U.S.

PRODUCER: Electra Bicycle Company
YEAR OF DEVELOPMENT: 2014
MAIN MATERIAL: aluminum frame

MANSORY Vitesse Rosé (Bentley)

The Vitesse Rosé is the basic model of the Bentley Continental GT Speed and is offered in a limited edition of three cars. It celebrated its world premiere at the Frankfurt Motor Show. The Vitesse Rosé features the exclusive MANSORY aerodynamics package, body components made of PU-RIM and a carbon fiber bonnet. The front and rear apron form a unit in connection with the side skirts, while LED daylight running lights integrated in the front apron render additional passive safety. A stainless steel exhaust system with two angular chrome tail pipes combines with the twelve-liter engine to deliver a thunderous roar. The interior features several luxury materials including hand-processed leather and aluminum pedals.

PRODUCER: MANSORY Design & Holding
YEAR OF DEVELOPMENT: 2009
MAIN MATERIAL: carbon

Penny Skateboards

The Penny Skateboards Pastel Collection was created to expand the range of classics with a fashionable twist. Pastel colors are incorporated throughout the plastic deck and the hardware components. The skateboard features 3-inch powder-coated Penny trucks, GOLD accent high tensile bolts and Penny Abec7 bearings. The Fresh

Prints collection is inspired by contemporary hip-hop music and graphic patterns with a nostalgic 1990s vibe. The collection includes a range of colorful boards, each with a different graphic on the bottom of the plastic deck. Penny Skateboards was founded by Ben Mackay and seeks to produce premium quality, ultra fun plastic skateboards.

PRODUCER: Penny Skateboards
YEAR OF DEVELOPMENT: 2014
MAIN MATERIAL: plastic

Commencal Supreme FR1

The design of the Supreme FR1 was inspired by the Hammer film company and its horror movies of the 1950s and 1960s. This explains the axes and ravens so prominent in the bike's graphics. The alloy hydroformed frame has a neon pink matt finish and a low center of gravity for greater stability. The tires are high roller, dual ply and the spokes are stainless steel. Commencal was launched in 2000 and has grown ever since, becoming an international brand by 2006. The first Supreme frames were introduced in 2005. A freeride version was launched in 2010 and a revised DH frame with a lower center of gravity in 2011.

DESIGN: Sebastien Caldas
PRODUCER: commencal
YEAR OF DEVELOPMENT: 2014
MAIN MATERIAL: alloy hydroformed 7005

Sebastien Caldas

GADGETS

Barbie Foot

The Barbie Foot combines the pink, frilly world of Barbie with the male world of table soccer. The conventional aluminum figurines have been replaced with Barbie figures and traditional masculine colors with pink to encourage users to question the traditional gendering of children's toys. Barbie Foot is a limited edition product, with only 8 available. The item was exhibited at the DMY International Design Festival in Berlin in June 2009 and was on sale at the Parisian store "Collette" later the same year. Since then, the product has appeared in many exhibitions and high-end stores including Selfridges in London. Chloé Ruchon studied at the Strasbourg School of Decorative Arts and designed Barbie Foot as one of her graduation pieces.

DESIGN: Chloé Ruchon
DISTRIBUTOR: Partnership with Bonzini and Mattel Brands Consumer Products
YEAR OF DEVELOPMENT: 2009
MAIN MATERIAL: Barbie, table soccer

Chloé Ruchon

Barbie foot

Leblon Beach Bat Set

Frescobol has been played on the beaches of Brazil since the 1940s, originally with heavy, clumsy paddles made of pine or cedar. Acquiring some wooden, handcrafted Frescobol beach bats on a trip to Bahia, long-term friends Harry Brantly and Max Leese were inspired to launch their own clothing and accessories brand with Frescobol providing the key lifestyle element. Each beach bat is handcrafted at Frescobol Carioca's Brazilian workshop where artisans select the best off-cut of woods such as Brazilian cherry, oak and rosewood. The Leblon beach bats comprise up to 13 pieces of wood and are finished with a surfboard resin and a choice of colorful neoprene grips including pink.

DESIGN: Harry Brantly, Max Leese
PRODUCER: Frescobol Carioca
YEAR OF DEVELOPMENT: 2009
MAIN MATERIAL: Brazilian wood off-cuts

Harry Brantly, Max Leese

PHOTOS: COURTESY OF THE PRODUCER

FRESCOBOL CARIOCA

RIO DE JANEIRO

Zippo Windproof Lighter

One of the most recognized brands in the world, Zippo was founded in the fall of 1932 by George G. Blaisdell in Bradford, Pennsylvania, where it has manufactured over 500 million windproof lighters. With the exception of improvements to the flint wheel and modifications in case finishes, the product remains unchanged. Like all Zippo lighters, the Zippo Classic in Pink Matte is backed by the company's famous lifetime guarantee – "It works, or we fix it free.™" Zippo's diverse product line includes lighter accessories, butane candle lighters, watches, fragrance, lifestyle accessories for men and a robust line of heat and flame products for outdoor enthusiasts.

PRODUCER: Zippo Manufacturing Company
YEAR OF DEVELOPMENT: 1933
MAIN MATERIAL: brass case with steel insert

PHOTOS: COURTESY OF THE PRODUCER

InLine Bobby

Bobby is the latest small Bluetooth Speakerphone by InLine®. The small speaker with integrated battery is intended for use while travelling and supports the hands-free function on mobile phones and smartphones. Once the initial setup is complete, pairing will happen automatically when Bluetooth is turned on. A second smartphone can also be paired with the device in a multipoint connection. The InLine Bobby features a protective cover in a choice of colors including pink, 30mm speakers with two resonance chambers, a Micro-USB charging cable and wrist strap. It weighs 60 grams and has a range of up to ten meters. Battery life is twelve hours for the speakerphone and three hours for music playback.

PRODUCER: Intos Electronic AG
YEAR OF DEVELOPMENT: 2014
MAIN MATERIAL: plastic, silicone

Diana F + Mr Pink

The Diana F + Mr Pink is a special edition of Lomography's iconic medium format camera. Lomography first released the Diana F + in 2007 as a loving recreation of the cult 1960s Diana camera which was famous for its vignetted photos and head-turning looks. Lomography added two shutter speeds, a pinhole function and a glamorous old-school flash amongst other features. This new edition finds its place among the growing family of Diana cameras. The 75mm lens features a zone focusing system and is easily removed to use the pinhole function. The hot pink color scheme represents a contemporary twist on a classic camera with a range of original and contemporary features.

PRODUCER: Lomography
YEAR OF DEVELOPMENT: 2009
MAIN MATERIAL: plastic

Victorinox Classic Pink

Small enough to use as a keyring but large enough to contain several useful tools, the Victorinox Pink Classic is a reinvention of a time-honored design. The unisex knife includes a range of features that make it suitable for many uses in both work and leisure contexts. Now available in a choice of colors, including bright pink, the pocket knife presents itself as a lifestyle accessory.

Its features include a knife, a nail file, a pair of scissors, a toothpick, a pair of tweezers and a keyring. Made of steel and plastic and only 58mm long, the Victorinox Pink Classic is small and lightweight. Founded in 1884, Victorinox has developed and expanded its range of products ever since, with this new classic series a recent addition to the family.

PRODUCER: Victorinox
YEAR OF DEVELOPMENT: 2008
MAIN MATERIAL: steel, plastic

Prynt Case

Prynt is the first instant camera case for smartphones. The user plugs in their phone, takes a photo and sees it printed within seconds. The case was designed to fit the latest Apple and Samsung phones with a physical connection to provide the best user experience possible. No ink cartridges are needed as, due to Zink technology, the color is already in the paper. The handle features a soft touch grip on the front and back that fits any hand. In order to be as thin as possible, the Prynt case folds itself when not in use, making it possible for users to carry it in their pockets or purses. The case also comes with an elegant leather strap.

Robin Barata

DESIGN: Robin Barata
PRODUCER: Prynt
YEAR OF DEVELOPMENT: 2014/2015
MAIN MATERIAL: plastic, leather

PHOTOS: COURTESY OF THE PRODUCER

IPHORIA

Berlin-based designer Milena Jäckel was inspired by her experience of urban life to create the label IPHORIA. Founded in 2012, the company produces fashionable cases, sleeves, bags and accessories for smartphones and tablets. Among her collection are several products available in pink. The Couleur Au Portable Candy

Pink case for the iPhone with a glossy finish is one such item. Others include a sleeve made from calfskin leather with a real fur pendant for the iPhone and the shock-absorbing TPU Bear Hug case. A more classic option is the Colour Blocking polycarbonate case in pink.

Milena Jäckel

DESIGN: Milena Jäckel
PRODUCER: IPHORIA
YEAR OF DEVELOPMENT: 2014
MAIN MATERIAL: TPU

instax mini 8

The FUJIFILM instax mini 8 uses Instant Color Film to print photos as soon as they are taken. The camera automatically determines the best brightness for taking a picture and informs the user of the suitable setting by lighting the corresponding lamp. There are four settings: indoors/night, cloudy/shade, sunny/slightly cloudy, sunny and bright.

A high-key mode allows the user to take photos with a softer impression. The shutter speed is fixed at 1/60 second and the flash, functional up to 2.7 meters, always fires. A variety of photo styles and film templates are available for the prints, which are credit-card sized (62mm x 46mm). There are seven color options including raspberry and grape.

PRODUCER: FUJIFILM
YEAR OF DEVELOPMENT: 2013
MAIN MATERIAL: plastic

urbanears headphones

Zinken are on-ear DJ headphones with large ear caps that eliminate noises in the surroundings, allowing the bass, mids and highs to be heard clearly. The dual-duty TurnCable with its 6.3mm and 3.5mm plugs eradicates the need for an adapter while the ZoundPlug enables the user to share music with a friend. The ear caps swivel and the handband can be adjusted for maximum comfort. A built-in microphone and remote can be used to answer phone calls on your device or fast forward or rewind your music. The headphones are fully collapsible for easy transportation. Plattan ADV is built with advanced features and sound, it comes with a washable headband, detachable cord with a built-in microphone and remote, as well as the ZoundPlug. Its 3D hinge makes it collapsible so it's easy to reduce the size. Among the available colors are two shades of pink: coral and jam.

PRODUCER: urbanears
YEAR OF DEVELOPMENT: 2014
MAIN MATERIAL: plastic

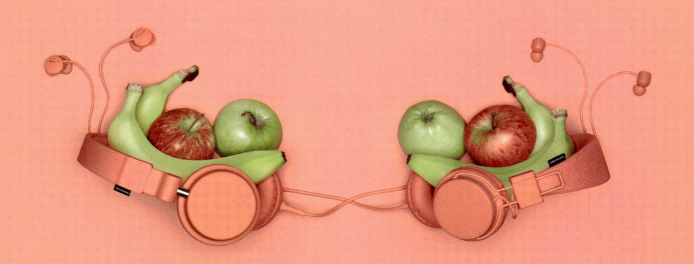

Sonicare DiamondClean

The Sonicare DiamondClean Pink Edition - Rechargeable sonic toothbrush by Philips has five different cleaning modes, including gum care, polish, sensitive and white. It can clean with up to 31,000 brushstrokes per minute and has a battery life of three weeks, based on two periods of two-minute brushings per day, on standard mode. An illuminated icon indicates the remaining battery life. The toothbrush comes with a glass charger and a fashionable travel case that is inspired by the look of a clutch - with the USB cord you can charge it at any laptop. The Sonicare is designed to clean along the gum line and in interdental spaces, as well as to remove plaque, stains and gently whiten the user's teeth. For easy and successful interdental space cleaning, the Sonicare AirFloss is also available in a matching Pink Edition.

PRODUCER: Philips
YEAR OF DEVELOPMENT: 2014
MAIN MATERIAL: ceramic finishing

Berlin Boombox

The Berlin Boombox was designed by Axel Pfaender and combines classic boombox style with modern audio technology. It is made from recycled corrugated cardboard and features a strong carrying handle and aluminum knob for power and volume control. The speakers and amplifier are German engineered by MIVOC Pro. It works with every smartphone and mp3 player, as well as laptops, tablets or gaming consoles, connecting to the device's headphone jack. The boombox comes as a kit consisting of a die-cut cardboard structure and all electronic parts. Assembly takes just a few minutes. Several colors and artists' editions are available.

DESIGN: Axel Pfaender
PRODUCER: Berlin Boombox
YEAR OF DEVELOPMENT: 2012
MAIN MATERIAL: cardboard

Axel Pfaender

PUBLIC SPACES

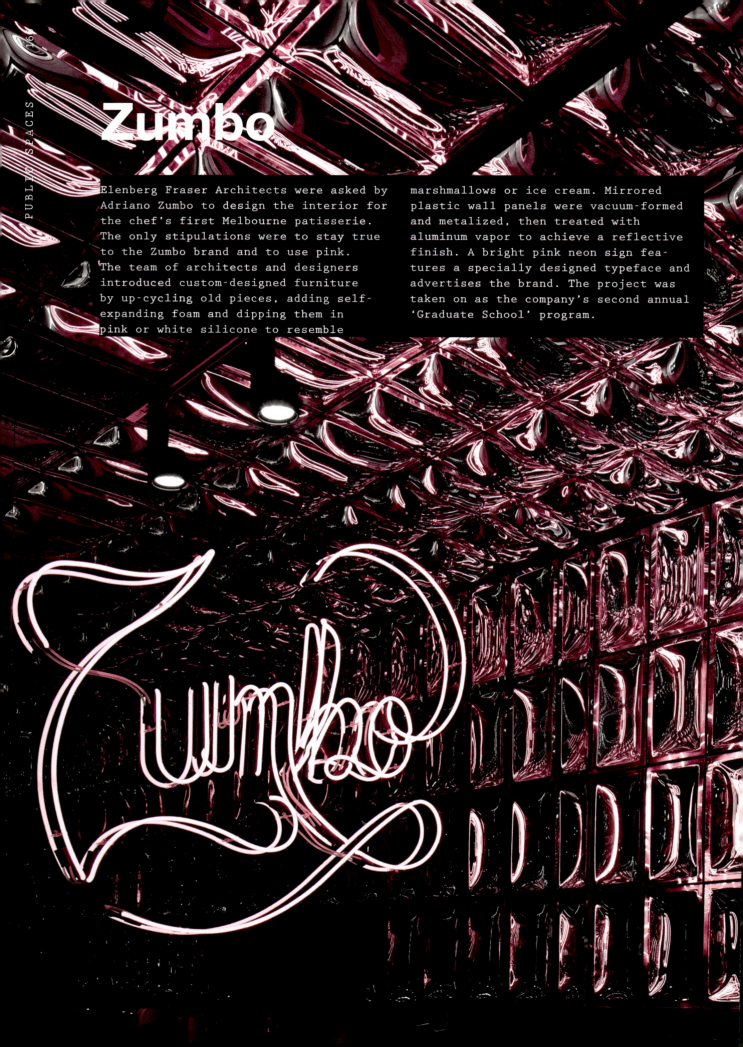

Zumbo

Elenberg Fraser Architects were asked by Adriano Zumbo to design the interior for the chef's first Melbourne patisserie. The only stipulations were to stay true to the Zumbo brand and to use pink. The team of architects and designers introduced custom-designed furniture by up-cycling old pieces, adding self-expanding foam and dipping them in pink or white silicone to resemble marshmallows or ice cream. Mirrored plastic wall panels were vacuum-formed and metalized, then treated with aluminum vapor to achieve a reflective finish. A bright pink neon sign features a specially designed typeface and advertises the brand. The project was taken on as the company's second annual 'Graduate School' program.

DESIGN: Elenberg Fraser Architects
YEAR OF DEVELOPMENT: 2013
MAIN MATERIAL (WALLS): vacuum-formed
polycarbonate panels with vacuum-metalized
finish
MAIN MATERIAL (FURNITURE): timber furniture,
triple expanding foam & silicone, vinyl seat
cushions

Flyknit

A temporary immersive installation was designed to completely transform the space of the Puro Sky Lounge on the 22nd floor of the iconic Europa-Center in Berlin. The design was developed in collaboration with onedotzero and consisted of two kilometers of tape arranged to create dynamic tension and optical effects that animated the whole environment. Fluorescent pink was one of two vivid colors used to create the display. The installation was part of a larger series of experience-based events produced by onedotzero and commissioned by Nike Brand Design Studio for the launch of the Nike Flyknit Lunar 2 collection of shoes.

DESIGN: Draisci Studio + onedotzero
YEAR OF DEVELOPMENT: 2014
MAIN MATERIAL: tape

Draisci Studio + onedotzero

PHOTOS: CHRISTIAN HELMUT HASSELBUSCH, CARLO DRAISCI (PORTRAIT DRAISCI STUDIO), MATT GRACE (PORTRAIT ONEDOTZERO)

Pink Caravan

Ainu Palmu's Pink Caravan was created for Lux Helsinki in 2013, a light festival of the City of Helsinki. Her installations carnivalized remarkable structures across central Helsinki, wrapping their façades in soft pink light. The idea was to give power back to the people. One building was chosen each evening of the festival, its illumination preceded by figures in pink performing at the structure during sunset. The locations included the Finnish National Theater, the Central Railway Station, the Helsinki University Main Library, the Bank of Finland and the Kaisaniemi Botanic Garden. The installation could also be seen at the Anti Festival in Kuopio, Finland, in September 2013.

DESIGN: Ainu Palmu for Lux Helsinki
YEAR OF DEVELOPMENT: 2013
MAIN MATERIAL: light

Ainu Palmu

Pink Bench

This 27-meter-long sculpture is located in the northern German town of Bremen. It serves as the visual highlight of a public square in the city center. Its form was inspired by the human spinal column, an image that has direct relevance to the health insurance company hkk that surrounds the square. The red brick colors of the surrounding historic architecture were digitally analyzed and used to create the particular shade of pink with which the bench is painted. As well as offering seating for visitors and residents of the city, the bench can also be used for bicycle storage. Designers Pierre Jorge Gonzalez and Judith Haase are based in Berlin.

DESIGN: Gonzalez Haase AAS
YEAR OF DEVELOPMENT: 2006
MAIN MATERIAL: zinced steel, painted wood

Gonzalez Haase AAS

Pink Balls

Pink Balls is a one-kilometer long ribbon-like installation of 170,000 resin balls suspended over Sainte-Catherine Street East in the Gay Village of Montreal. It is part of the transformation of the street into a pedestrian mall over the summer. The plastic balls, in three different sizes and five subtle shades of pink, are strung together with bracing wire, crisscrossing the street and stretching through tree branches at varying heights. The installation has been deployed in nine sections, each section displaying its own unique pattern. By integrating the community into the project, Pink Balls has increased the appeal among both local visitors and tourists, becoming a catalyst for economic and social development.

DESIGN: Claude Cormier et Associés
YEAR OF DEVELOPMENT: 2012-2014
MAIN MATERIAL: pink plastic balls

Claude Cormier et Associés

PHOTOS: MARC CRAMER (P. 175 & B. L.), GUILLAUME PARADIS (PP. 174, 175 B. R.), WILLIEN PORTRAIT)

Fly Tower

BaO was invited by the Beijing Design Week to design and build an installation for the 2014 Dashilar BJDW pop-up forum space. The Fly Tower was the result, a contemporary iconic structure inserted into the middle of the turn-of-the-century Guild House QuanYeChang. The ground floor was dedicated to the "Making futures" forums and informal discussions while the upper body of the tower was used as a support for a vertical multimedia exhibition unfolding on the second and third floors of the venue. The bright pink tower, in radical contrast with its art-deco surroundings, advocated a pop, optimistic and playful subversion of contemporary architectural icons.

DESIGN: BaO architects
YEAR OF DEVELOPMENT: 2014
MAIN MATERIAL: steel structure, pink cloth

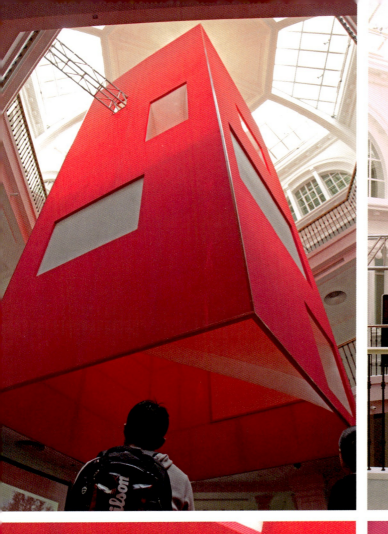

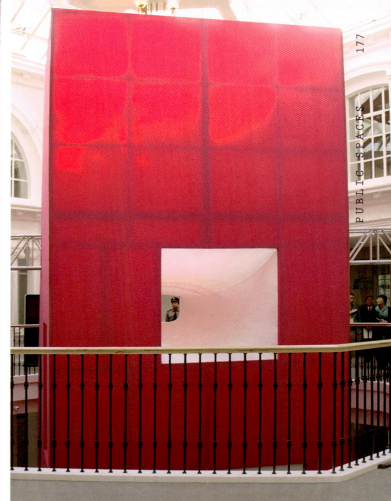

PHOTOS: QUAN YE CHANG/COURTESY OF THE ARCHITECTS

Benjamin Beller/BaO

Dynamorph

Dynamorph was designed for the exhibition on Shamanism for the International Cultural Institute during the Venice Biennale 2014. The pink pavilion exhibits Nepalese shamanic artifacts and was created to visualize 'Urja', the force or energy that the shamans attempt to control through their practices. Positioned between the exhibits and the room, Dynamorph is an iso-surface that envelops the visitors and forms a surreal, mystical cave that interfaces between the present and the past. The branching and flowing geometry of Dynamorph evokes the symbolism of roots, trunks and branches that form the three worlds of shamanism.

DESIGN: Orproject
YEAR OF DEVELOPMENT: 2014
MAIN MATERIAL: paper

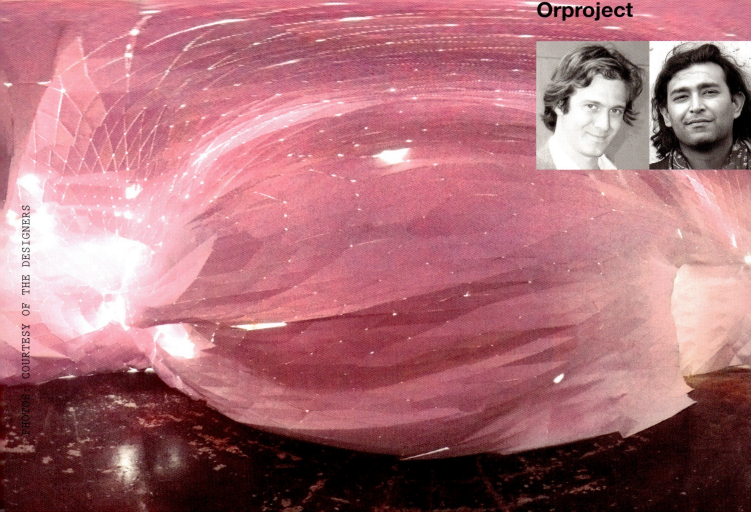

Orproject

Pink Punch

Pink Punch was created for the 2013 and 2014 Jardins de Métis International Garden Festival in Grand-Métis, Quebec, Canada. The installation aims to attract visitors off the beaten path by its striking color, through the shaped garden rooms, and into the forest. This "pinkscape" is made from natural rubber pink latex rope wrapped around each tree at a height of three meter, then wound until it reaches the ground. At the ground, the rope then continues to wind around the base of the tree to a radial distance of one meter. When a small cluster of trees are wrapped to their bases, the rope then envelops them all, creating a communal seating area at the base of each tree.

DESIGN: Michaela Macleod, Nicholas Croft
YEAR OF DEVELOPMENT: 2013
MAIN MATERIAL: natural latex rubber rope

**Michaela Macleod,
Nicholas Croft**

PHOTOS: LOUISE TANGUAY/FESTIVAL INTERNATIONAL DE JARDINS/LES JARDINS DE MÉTIS. MICHAELA MACLEOD (DRAWING). NICHOLAS CROFT (P. 181 A. (SMALL PHOTO)

Spring Forest

Spring Forest was commissioned by Clerkenwell Design Week and installed in St James' Church garden. It comprises a group of thin red and pink poles, 3.5 meters high, topped by 100 umbrellas to resemble a forest of giant poppy flowers. The scaffolding components are red and clad in foam to blend with the 'flowers'. Light filters through the canopy to create a unique environment beneath, where the open grid allows social interaction as well as privacy. The brief for the project called for a low-budget temporary intervention and resourceful use of sponsor Fulton Umbrellas to stimulate the expected crowd of 35,000 visitors.

DESIGN: Draisci Studio
FABRICATOR: Clockwork Scenery
YEAR OF DEVELOPMENT: 2012
MAIN MATERIAL: umbrellas, foam-cladded scaffolding poles

Draisci Studio

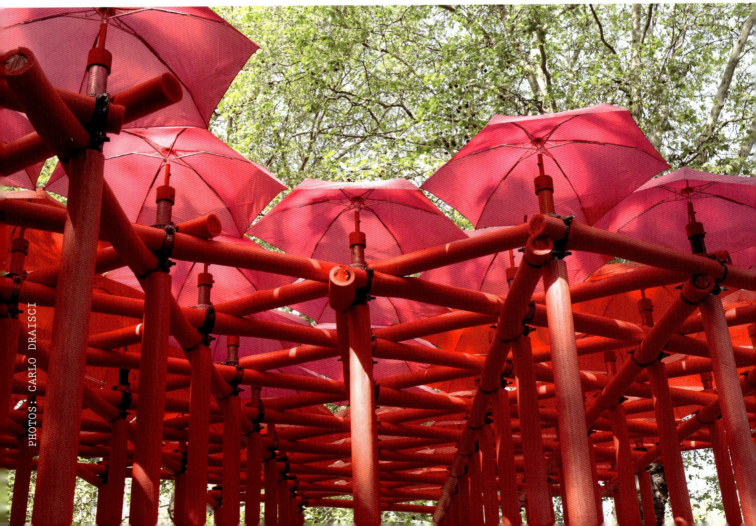

Sugar Beach

Located at the foot of Lower Jarvis Street adjacent to the Redpath Sugar Factory of Toronto, the 8,500 square meter Sugar Beach park is the first public space visitors see as they travel along Queens Quay from the central waterfront. The park features three distinct components - an urban beach, a plaza space, and a tree-lined promenade running diagonally through the park. Sugar as concept was used to establish a language for many of the elements throughout the park, from the red and white bedrock candy stripes on the park's two outcroppings, the soft confection-like pink of the umbrellas, and even the candy cane pattern on the stainless steel ventilation pipes to the fountain mechanical vault concealed under the promenade.

DESIGN: Claude Cormier et Associés
YEAR OF DEVELOPMENT: 2010
MAIN MATERIAL: fiberglass umbrellas,
granite bedrock with thermoplastic stripes

Claude Cormier et Associés

PHOTOS: NICOLA BETTS (PP. 184, 185 M.B.), EASTERN CONSTRUCTION (P. 185 A.), WILL LEW (PORTRAIT)

Open House

Artist Matthew Mazzotta, the Coleman Center for the Arts and the people of York (Alabama) teamed up to transform a blighted property in York's downtown area into a new public art project. They used the materials from the original house and the land it occupied to build a new smaller house where the old one used to be. The appearance is deceptive, however, as the structure can be transformed into an open-air theater that seats 100 people and is free to the public. Spending most of its time in the form of a house surrounded by a public park, the theater is opened up when the community wants to enjoy shows, plays, movies or other events.

DESIGN: Matthew Mazzotta
YEAR OF DEVELOPMENT: 2013
MAIN MATERIAL: materials reclaimed from an abandoned house

PHOTOS: COURTESY OF THE DESIGNER

Situation Room

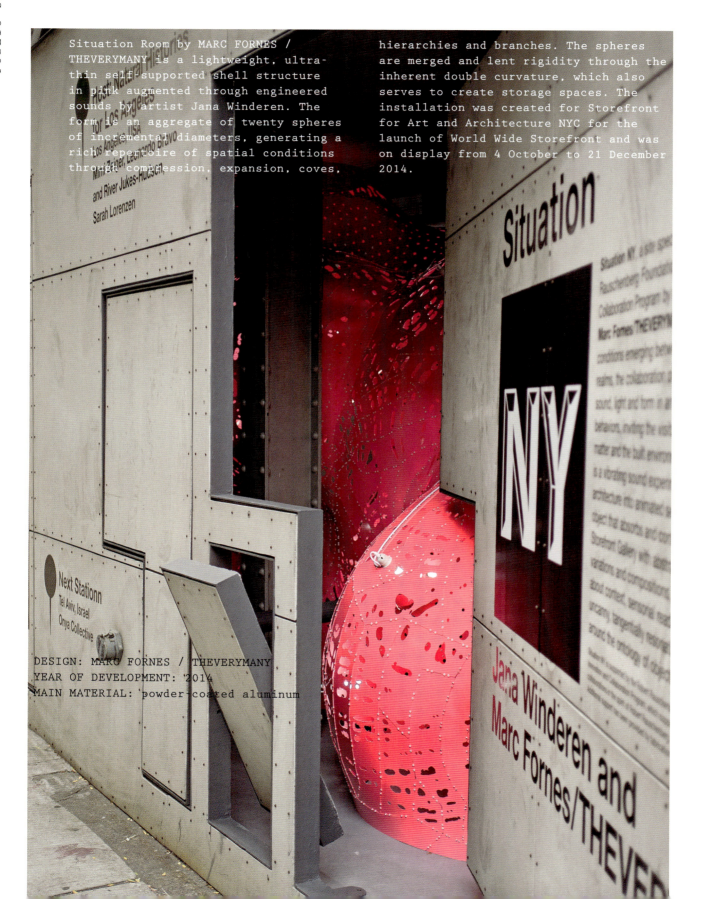

Situation Room by MARC FORNES / THEVERYMANY is a lightweight, ultra-thin self-supported shell structure in pink augmented through engineered sounds by artist Jana Winderen. The form is an aggregate of twenty spheres of incremental diameters, generating a rich repertoire of spatial conditions through compression, expansion, coves, hierarchies and branches. The spheres are merged and lent rigidity through the inherent double curvature, which also serves to create storage spaces. The installation was created for Storefront for Art and Architecture NYC for the launch of World Wide Storefront and was on display from 4 October to 21 December 2014.

DESIGN: MARC FORNES / THEVERYMANY
YEAR OF DEVELOPMENT: 2014
MAIN MATERIAL: powder-coated aluminum

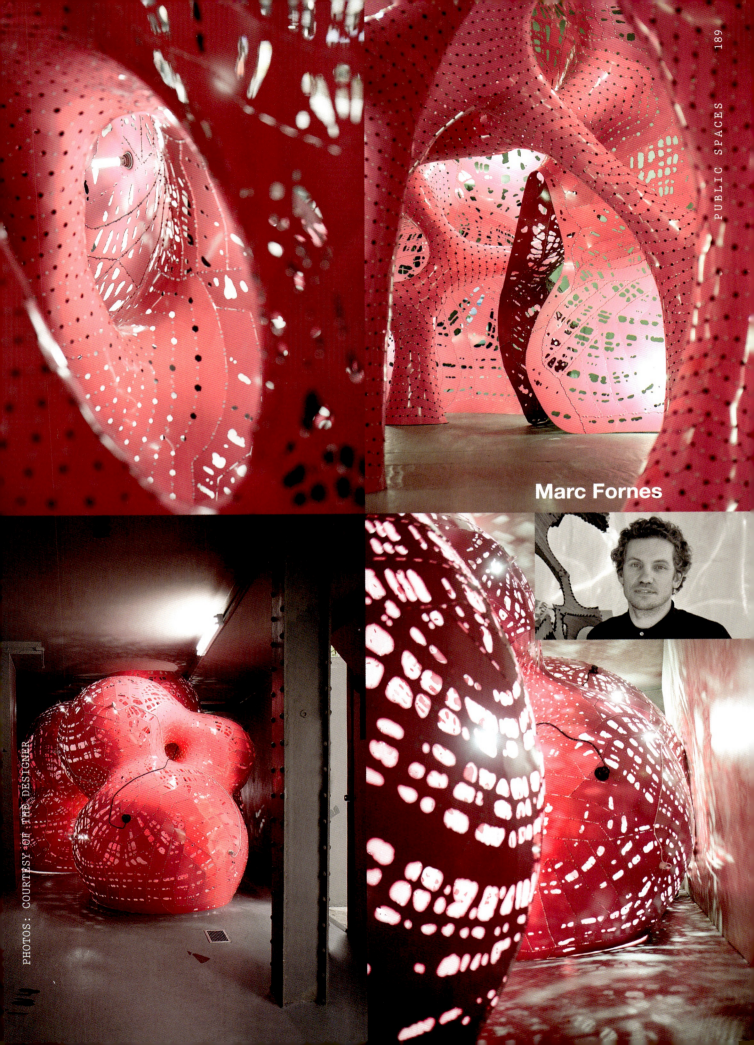

Marc Fornes

Index

Imprint

The Deutsche Nationalbibliothek lists
this publication in the Deutsche
Nationalbibliografie; detailed
bibliographic data are available on
the Internet at http://dnb.dnb.de

ISBN 978-3-03768-196-1
© 2015 by Braun Publishing AG
www.braun-publishing.ch

1st edition 2015

Editor and layout: Manuela Roth
Translations and text editing:
Judith Vonberg
Art direction: Michaela Prinz, Berlin